THE BOOK OF THE TWELVE

CASCADE COMPANIONS

The Christian theological tradition provides an embarrassment of riches: from Scripture to modern scholarship, we are blessed with a vast and complex theological inheritance. And yet this feast of traditional riches is too frequently inaccessible to the general reader.

The Cascade Companions series addresses the challenge by publishing books that combine academic rigor with broad appeal and readability. They aim to introduce nonspecialist readers to that vital storehouse of authors, documents, themes, histories, arguments, and movements that comprise this heritage with brief yet compelling volumes.

RECENT TITLES IN THIS SERIES:

The Canaanites by Mary Ellen Buck
Deuteronomy by Jack R. Lundblom
David by Benjamin J. M. Johnson
Amos, Hosea, and Micah by Jack R. Lundblom
Practicing Lament by Rebekah Eklund
Approaching Job by Andrew Zack Lewis
Jesus and the Empire of God by Warren Carter
Reading John by Christopher W. Skinner
Reading Acts by Joshua W. Jipp
Reading Paul by Michael Gorman
Reading 1 Corinthians by J. Brian Tucker
Reading Philippians by Nijay K. Gupta
A Companion to Philemon by Lewis Brogdon
Hebrews in Social-Scientific Perspective by David A. deSilva
A Companion to the Book of Revelation by David L. Matthews
Scripture's Knowing by Dru Johnson
Theological Interpretation of Scripture by Stephen Fowl
The Rule of Faith by Everett Ferguson
The Second-Century Apologists by Alvyn Pettersen
Origen by Ronald E. Heine
Athanasius of Alexandria by Lois Farag
A Guide to St Symeon the New Theologian by Hannah Hunt
Rudolph Bultmann by David W. Congdon

THE BOOK OF THE TWELVE

By BETH M. STOVELL
and DAVID J. FULLER

CASCADE *Books* · Eugene, Oregon

THE BOOK OF THE TWELVE

Cascade Companions

Copyright © 2022 Beth M. Stovell and David J. Fuller. All rights reserved. Except for brief quotations in critical publications or reviews, no part of this book may be reproduced in any manner without prior written permission from the publisher. Write: Permissions, Wipf and Stock Publishers, 199 W. 8th Ave., Suite 3, Eugene, OR 97401.

Cascade Books
An Imprint of Wipf and Stock Publishers
199 W. 8th Ave., Suite 3
Eugene, OR 97401

www.wipfandstock.com

PAPERBACK ISBN: 978-1-7252-6298-0
HARDCOVER ISBN: 978-1-7252-6299-7
EBOOK ISBN: 978-1-7252-6300-0

Cataloguing-in-Publication data:

Names: Stovell, Beth M., author. | Fuller, David J., author.

Title: The book of the twelve / by Beth M. Stovell and David J. Fuller.

Description: Eugene, OR: Cascade Books, 2022 | Series: Cascade Companions | Includes bibliographical references and index.

Identifiers: ISBN 978-1-7252-6298-0 (paperback) | ISBN 978-1-7252-6299-7
(hardcover) | ISBN 978-1-7252-6300-0 (ebook)

Subjects: LCSH: Bible—Minor prophets—Criticism, interpretation, etc. | Bible—Criticism, interpretation, etc. | Bible—Theology

Classification: BS1560 S76 2022 (print) | BS1560 (ebook)

05/23/22

CONTENTS

Acknowledgments · vii
Abbreviations · ix

1. Is the Twelve "the Twelve"? An Introduction · 1
2. Theological Approaches to the Twelve · 13
3. Restoration of the Davidic Monarchy · 29
4. Repentance and Return · 52
5. The Day of the Lord · 70
6. Creation, Nature, and Land · 91
7. Theodicy and Hope · 110
8. Literary, Linguistic, and Wisdom Approaches to the Twelve · 130
9. How Was the Twelve Written and Formed? · 142

Bibliography · 165
Author Index · 177
Scripture Index · 181

ACKNOWLEDGMENTS

David would particularly like to thank his wife and his son for all their encouragement and support throughout the writing process. Experiencing the birth of their first child near the end of the journey of writing this book (and during the teaching of a course on the Minor Prophets) was a rich and joyous blessing. David is also grateful to his co-author, Beth Stovell, both for the initial invitation to write this book together and also for her guidance and mentorship along the way.

Besides thanking her co-author, David, for the wonderful experience of collaboration on this project, Beth would like to thank Mark Boda, who so many years ago introduced her to thinking about the Twelve prophets as "the Twelve." She would like to thank her colleagues Colin Toffelmire, Daniel Timmer, and George Athas, who were working with her on another volume on the Twelve (*Theodicy and Hope in the Book of the Twelve*, T. & T. Clark Bloomsbury, 2021) at the same time as this book. For many years, they have co-chaired together the Institute

Acknowledgments

for Biblical Research "The Book of the Twelve Prophets in Biblical Scholarship" Research Group. Through their friendship and collaboration, they have expanded her view of the Twelve. Finally, Beth could not complete a project like this without the support of her husband, Jon Stovell, and her kids, Elena and Atticus. They inspire her to see the world in new ways and to engage life as an ever-unfolding adventure!

ABBREVIATIONS

AcBib	Academia Biblica
AcT	*Acta Theologica*
ANEM	Ancient Near East Monographs/Monografías sobre el Antiquo Cercano Oriente
AOAT	Alter Orient und Altes Testament
BAR	*Biblical Archaeology Review*
BBR	*Bulletin for Biblical Research*
BETL	Bibliotheca Ephemeridum Theologicarum Lovaniensium
BLS	Bible and Literature Series
Bib	*Biblica*
BibInt	Biblical Interpretation Series
BZAW	Beihefte zur Zeitschrift für die alttestamentliche Wissenschaft

Abbreviations

CBET	Contributions to Biblical Exegesis and Theology
CBQ	*Catholic Biblical Quarterly*
Colloq	*Colloquium*
CTJ	*Calvin Theological Journal*
CTQ	*Concordia Theological Quarterly*
CurBR	*Currents in Biblical Research*
ETL	*Ephemerides Theologicae Lovanienses*
ExpTim	*Expository Times*
FAT	Forschungen zum Alten Testament
FRLANT	Forschungen zur Religion und Literatur des Alten und Neuen Testaments
HBM	Hebrew Bible Monographs
HBT	*Horizons in Biblical Theology*
IBC	Interpretation: A Bible Commentary for Teaching and Preaching
Int	*Interpretation*
JBL	*Journal of Biblical Literature*
JBQ	*Jewish Bible Quarterly*
JETS	*Journal of the Evangelical Theological Society*
JSOT	*Journal for the Study of the Old Testament*
JSOTSup	Journal for the Study of the Old Testament Supplement Series
LHBOTS	The Library of Hebrew Bible/Old Testament Studies

NICOT	New International Commentary on the Old Testament
NIVAC	NIV Application Commentary
NSBT	New Studies in Biblical Theology
OBO	Orbis Biblicus et Orientalis
OTE	*Old Testament Essays*
RBS	Resources for Biblical Study
RevExp	*Review and Expositor*
SEÅ	*Svensk exegetisk årsbok*
SHBC	Smyth & Helwys Bible Commentary
SSN	Studia Semitica Neerlandica
SymS	Symposium Series
Them	*Themelios*
TJT	*Toronto Journal of Theology*
VT	*Vetus Testamentum*
VTSup	Supplements to Vetus Testamentum
ZAW	*Zeitschrift für die alttestamentliche Wissenschaft*

1

IS THE TWELVE "THE TWELVE"?

An Introduction

INTRODUCTION

WHILE CHATTING WITH A New Testament scholar years ago, the scholar asked us, "What do you study?" We responded, "The Twelve." He replied, "The Twelve of what?" This scholar's question is at the core of our book. When we say "the Twelve," what are we referring to and why does it matter? In its most basic sense, a part of the answer is straightforward. We use the phrases "the Twelve" or "the Twelve Prophets" or "the Book of the Twelve Prophets" to refer to the twelve short prophetic books in the Hebrew Bible from Hosea to Malachi also sometimes referred to as "the Minor Prophets": Hosea, Joel, Amos, Obadiah, Jonah, Micah, Nahum, Habakkuk, Zephaniah, Haggai,

Zechariah, and Malachi. While the term "the Minor Prophets" describes these twelve books in terms of their small size in comparison to "the Major Prophets," Isaiah, Jeremiah, Ezekiel, and Daniel,[1] the term "the Twelve" and its counterparts emphasize the *connections* between these twelve books, treating them as a single "Book." This is why we sometimes hear the term "the Book of the Twelve Prophets." This term points directly to the idea that reading these Twelve prophets together is similar to reading a single prophetic book like Isaiah or Ezekiel.

Yet this raises a logical follow-up question: why would we think of these twelve books as a single book? What evidence do we have for thinking this way about them? This introductory chapter explores both the history of this approach and evidence related to why we might think of these twelve works as a single "book." It will also chart the exploration of the themes and approaches to the Twelve found throughout the rest of the book. We end this chapter by offering definitions to key terms that we will use along the way.

HISTORY AND EVIDENCE CONCERNING THE "BOOK OF THE TWELVE"

First, let us explore the history of the term "Book of the Twelve" and the evidence for treating the Twelve as a single work. While describing these twelve prophets as "the Book of the Twelve" is relatively new in biblical scholarship, emerging in the late 1970s and early 1980s

---

1. The largest of the Twelve are Zechariah and Hosea with fourteen chapters each. The rest of the Twelve tend to be shorter, ranging from nine chapters in Amos to a single chapter of Obadiah. In comparison, Isaiah tops the Major Prophets with sixty-six chapters. Yet one could point out that Daniel is comparable in length to the Minor Prophets with only twelve chapters.

and continuing into today, this approach to the Twelve is based on historical evidence dating to the time between the Old and New Testaments, the time of the Second Temple in Jerusalem, and traced to language used by some of our earliest interpreters of the Bible.

One reason for viewing the Twelve as a single book comes from archaeological evidence. We have ancient manuscripts of these twelve prophets where parts of them are placed together in a single scroll. There may be debate about whether this is because the books were read together intentionally or simply due to the small size of these books and the difficulty in finding the resources to make scrolls. Nonetheless, the location of the twelve prophetic books in a single scroll would impact how those reading the scroll understood the links between the different books. For example, a cursory glance at the first verses of Hosea, Amos, and Micah shows us that these books speak to roughly the same time period, as these prophets lived during the same set of kings: Uzziah, Jotham, Ahaz, and Hezekiah in the southern kingdom of Judah and Jeroboam in the northern kingdom of Israel. Meanwhile, examining recurring motifs and catchwords show how different books show signs of links with one another.

Describing these books as "The Twelve Prophets" is also found in very early ancient texts. Both Josephus and 4 Ezra are dated to the first century CE, around the time of Jesus, and these authors both count the Twelve as one book.[2] Other Jewish traditions treat the Twelve as a collected unit, as we see in the Babylonian Talmud and the notes of the Masoretes, who put together the pronunciation markings for the original Hebrew text of the Old Testament. We call this the Masoretic Text or MT.[3] Early church fathers also spoke

2. Nogalski, *Micah–Malachi*, 490.
3. For the Babylonian Talmud, see *b. B. Bat.* 13b–15a. For more

THE BOOK OF THE TWELVE

of the Twelve as a single unit. In the prologue to his translation of the Old Testament, Jerome (347–420 CE) points to the tradition that "the Twelve is one book."[4] It seems likely that Jerome was sharing the tradition that he learned from the Jewish rabbis who taught him Hebrew.[5]

Scholars who study these twelve prophets using this notion of "The Twelve" further demonstrate the shared nature of these prophetic texts by pointing to a wide array of unifying elements that join the individual books of the Twelve to one another, including: catchwords, themes, motifs, repetition in endings and beginnings, shared metaphorical imagery, inner-biblical allusion, and theological connections. For example, the Twelve has many examples of lion imagery, including Hos 5:14–15; 11:10; 13:7–8; Amos 1:2; and Joel 3:16.[6] This imagery shows striking similarities and development throughout the Twelve. Not only does this lion imagery show connections between these books within the Twelve, it also shows dependence on similar inner-biblical allusions, including alluding to Gen 49:8–12, where Judah is crouching like a lion, and Num 23:21–24, which echoes this imagery in Balaam's oracles. Elements like this lion imagery function as unifying elements across the Twelve and between the Twelve and other parts of the Old Testament.

Scholars of "The Twelve" also frequently explore the formation and composition of "the Twelve" (these terms will be explored in more detail below). They may seek to trace the development of the books and how they came to be joined with one another. As noted, some of the

---

on this, see Nogalski, *Micah–Malachi*, 490.

4. *Biblia Sacra Vulgata*, 2:1374.

5. Nogalski, *Micah–Malachi*, 490–91.

6. van Hecke, "Leonine Metaphors in the Twelve Prophets," 387–402.

prophets in the Twelve were overlapping prophets due to their shared time period. For this reason, Hosea, Amos, Micah, and Zephaniah are sometimes called the "Book of the Four" and are seen as one of the earlier collections that were eventually joined at a subsequent stage to the rest of the Twelve prophets, who wrote at later times. Scholars will also speak of the Twelve as having a first and second half and debate on which of the books form the literary center. This is related to the broad time period represented in the Twelve. The earliest of the books in the Twelve—such as Amos, Hosea, and Micah—were written in the eighth century, when the Assyrians loomed large as the nearby national power, prior to the Babylonian exile (a period we thus call "pre-exilic"). The final books of the Twelve—like Zechariah, Haggai, and Malachi—were written during the Persian period, after the Israelites had returned from exile (which we call "post-exilic"). While the twelve books are not perfectly in chronological order, the first half of the Twelve tend to be closer to the start of this time period and the second half of the Twelve tend to be closer to the end of this time period. Discussions of formation and composition focus on how these books, ranging across such a broad span of time, came to be collected and joined to form the "Book of the Twelve" we know today.

Exploring the composition of the Twelve includes exploring the different versions of the texts themselves that we find in various versions of our biblical text. This includes comparing the Masoretic Text (MT, a Hebrew version of the Old Testament) with the LXX (Septuagint, a Greek translation of the Hebrew Old Testament text) and with the Vulgate (a Latin translation of the Hebrew Old Testament text). The order of the books within the Twelve differs in these translations, which is one of the discussion points about the history of the Twelve. Chapter 9 of this book will explore in greater detail the Twelve's process of formation and composition and the impact of these different translations on understanding the Twelve.

So why does this matter? How does reading the Twelve as a single literary unit rather than as individual books change what we see when we look at these books? First, reading the Twelve as a literary unit offers the ability to follow themes across the Twelve. Second, reading the Twelve in this way advances our understanding of the theology and purpose of the Twelve. These two elements of the themes of the Twelve and their impact on the theology and the purpose of the Twelve will frame the rest of this book.

STRUCTURE AND CONTENT OF THIS BOOK

In terms of structure, our book can be divided into two main parts: in Part 1, chapters 2–7 explore theological themes in the Twelve; in Part 2, chapters 8–9 examine topics and approaches to the Twelve. Each chapter explains the contours of the theme or topic, explores specific books in the Twelve where this theme or topic arises, and then offers a section called "Viewing the Big Picture." This final section draws together the analysis of specific books to discuss what this means for the Twelve overall. Each chapter ends with a series of reflection questions useful for exploring the content of each chapter further, whether readers are using this book for personal study or for study in a group setting.

Our book begins with an introduction to the theology of the Twelve in chapter 2. This chapter explores three different ways that scholars have explored theology in the Twelve:

- seeking an integral theological center to the Twelve

- examining elements that create continuity in the Twelve, and
- exploring specific theological topics within the Twelve.

This overview of theology of the Twelve provides the foundations for the specific exploration of themes in the Twelve in chapters 3–7.

Chapter 3 explores the theme of Davidic kingship in the Twelve. It examines the tensions that arise in the presentation of the hope of a future Davidic king compared to the rule of God as the ultimate king. This chapter explores the complexity of different perspectives on interpreting this theme of restoration of the Davidic monarchy and its impact on Israel's enduring hopes for the future.

Chapter 4 returns to the theme of restoration in the Twelve. However, instead of focusing on the restoration of the Davidic monarchy, this chapter examines the theme of repentance and return where God offers Israel restoration with him if they will only turn from their wicked ways and turn towards him again. This chapter highlights in the Twelve both the array of sinful actions and beliefs that have caused Israel to need this repentance and the array of beautiful imagery of blessings in their restoration to God, if they return to him.

Chapter 5 examines the theme of the "Day of the Lord" in the Twelve. The chapter first clarifies what counts as a "Day of the Lord" reference. Scholars have ranged widely in what they consider to be a reference to this "Day." Some scholars require the entire phrase word-for-word to count it as an example, while others are satisfied with any inferred notion of the "Day." This chapter shows that the Day of the Lord is not a completely consistent concept in the Twelve, as it is sometimes a positive and other times a negative one. Yet the concept does have one consistent element throughout the Twelve: the Day of the Lord is *a day when* Yhwh *intervenes*. This intervention may be perceived as positive and characterized by blessings or negative and characterized by punishment. Yet in either case, the goal is for the readers to listen to the Lord, respond to his calls, and expect his future intervention. This chapter touches on how this picture of the Day of the Lord in the Twelve shapes this concept in the New Testament.

Chapter 6 shifts from the focus of previous chapters on God's relationship with Israel as a people to focus on God's relationship with Israel as the land and the creatures that inhabit it. This chapter provides an overview of select places that nature shows up in the Twelve, using the categories of (1) the health of the land as an indicator of divine favor, (2) themes of creation and uncreation in the Twelve, (3) celestial imagery in the Twelve, (4) animal imagery in the Twelve, and (5) ecological readings of the Twelve. The chapter reflects God's care for nature in the Twelve and how what happens in the natural world in the Twelve often reflects what happens between God and his people.

Chapter 7 explores the topic of theodicy and hope in the Twelve. Many scholars see theodicy and hope as a theme that integrates the other themes we mentioned above. Explorations of theodicy and hope ask tough questions about how God deals with suffering and the need for justice and how God offers hope amidst suffering to his people. The chapter shows how the Twelve, when read as a whole, offers an overarching story of the hope of God's justice enacted against Israel's enemies and the expectation of God's presence, rule, and restoration.

Whereas chapters 3–7 focus on themes in the Twelve, chapters 8–9 explore hermeneutical strategies for reading the Twelve. Chapter 8 examines a variety of approaches to the Twelve, including literary, linguistic, and wisdom approaches. This chapter traces the development of these different ways of interpreting the Twelve. It shows both the complexities and opportunities that arise from using these diverse methods.

Chapter 9 ends where chapter 1 began: exploring what makes "the Twelve" the Twelve. It provides a more detailed overview of the different theories concerning the formation and composition of the Twelve and the implications of that formation process. This chapter thus functions as a deeper explanation of the discussion we began in chapter 1 as well as a conclusion to the entire book.

DEFINITIONS

In order to have greater clarity along the way as we explore the Twelve, it is helpful to first define some of the academic terms used in this book. Let's start by exploring the related terms "editing/editorial," "redaction/redactional," "composition/compositional," and "formation/formational." We can begin by thinking more broadly about how we received the Bible we have today. While it is common in many churches today to speak about the Bible as though its books were simply written by a prophet or gospel writer and then placed in the Bible we have today, the process by which we received our present Bible is more complicated.

First, it is helpful to realize that all of our modern books go through a process of editing before they are published. Even the best writers have editors who help them revise the original manuscript until it is refined into its final form that is published and read. Many people have contributed to producing the book that we can buy off a shelf in a bookstore.

In the ancient world, this process was even more extensive because the ancient world prioritized sharing by speech over sharing by writing (oral transmission over written transmission). Stories and prophetic words were kept safe by ancient storytellers over centuries by practicing these stories and prophetic words again and again in front of listeners who often could not write themselves. When these stories and prophetic words were finally written down, it was often because those storytellers were in danger of dying out. They feared that the stories and words of the prophet would then be lost.

Writing these traditions down was often done more like a process of scrapbooking today than like a single author writing a book. Scrapbooks from someone's university years might include pictures the person took themselves alongside pictures from others. The scrapbook might have fragments of notes written by friends or common sayings or memories from friends alongside the person's own. The ancient editorial process, which we sometimes call "redaction," was similar to this scrapbooking process. Ancient editors brought together stories or writings from others, memories of events, and other oral traditions. They tied these pieces together into a coherent whole with different editorial additions. In this process, they sought God's direction to honor best the traditions they were inheriting. Similar to captions in a scrapbook, editors or redactors may add the dates when a prophet received a message from God or list the kings during the prophet's lifetime. In the case of the Book of the Twelve, such editors might extend this work past editing in Amos or Micah as individual books to the broader work of joining Amos with Hosea, Micah, and Zephaniah, connecting them to one another. We use the term "composition" to discuss the entire process from editing a specific individual book to joining the different books within the Twelve to one another through various forms of editorial binding. We may also use the language of "formation" to describe this process.

Two further terms that arise in discussions of composition are "diachronic" and "synchronic." Diachronic (from the Greek *dia* meaning "across" and *chronos* meaning "time") is a way of reading the Bible that focuses on the history of how a biblical book came to be. Diachronic scholars look for the layers of redaction that point to the different time periods of writing and editing that shaped the way the Twelve, or any specific book in the Twelve, became what we have today. In contrast, synchronic (from the Greek *syn* meaning "same" and *chronos* meaning "time") focuses on the final version of the text we have in Scripture. These synchronic approaches use methods to examine the text that do not explore the backstory of the text's formation, but instead focus on literary or linguistic aspects of the text. We will discuss synchronic approaches to the Twelve in chapter 8 and diachronic approaches to the Twelve in chapter 9 in more detail. Hopefully this introduction gives us a starting place for these subsequent deeper discussions.

CONCLUSION

This book is intended to lead the reader on a journey through the themes and topics that make the Twelve unique. In this book, we offer both a bird's eye view of the big picture of the Twelve and deep dives into the details of that picture. Our hope is that this journey will help the Twelve come alive for readers and speak in new and fresh ways.

REFLECTION QUESTIONS:

1. What are some reasons that modern scholars might call the short twelve prophets at the end of the Old Testament "the Twelve"?

2. What are factors scholars believe unify the Twelve? Do you find them convincing thus far? Why or why not?

3. What interests you about studying the Twelve?

2

THEOLOGICAL APPROACHES TO THE TWELVE

INTRODUCTION

As DISCUSSED IN CHAPTER 1, one of the unique advantages of reading the Book of the Twelve as a single unified book is the way it offers added dimensions of theological understanding. Yet many different questions and issues can arise when we study the Book of the Twelve theologically. This chapter will look at the ways that scholars have read the Twelve theologically in the past three decades. In doing so, we will introduce the specific themes that are covered in more detail in the subsequent chapters of this book. The theological study of the Twelve can be grouped into three major categories: (1) proposals for an integral theological center to the Twelve, (2) exploration of theological elements that lend continuity to the Twelve, and (3) studies that focus on specific theological topics.

ELEMENTS THAT ARE CENTRAL TO THE TWELVE

Some scholars believe that there is *one central theme* that unites the Twelve. In other words, they would argue that their particular theme provides something of an interpretive "key" that unlocks the function of the Twelve as a whole.

James D. Nogalski, in "Reading the Book of the Twelve Theologically" (2007) lays the groundwork for reading the Book of the Twelve as a literary unity. He begins with the problem of faithfully appropriating the multivalent dialectic between judgment and deliverance in the Twelve.[1] He notes that six of the books of the Twelve (Hosea, Amos, Micah, Zephaniah, Haggai, and Zech 1–8) have superscriptions that assign them to a clear historical context,[2] and further argues that four of the other books (Nahum, Habakkuk, Jonah, and Malachi) fit clearly into the implied historical setting of the surrounding books. Meanwhile, the two remaining books (Joel and Obadiah) appear to be crafted to fit with their canonical neighbors thematically, particularly in terms of their discussions of the Day of the LORD.[3] Nogalski also notes that catchwords function to create thematic links between adjacent books, and documents four types of these links: "juxtaposition of promise against judgment," "parallels between the fates of two entities," "reappearance of entities in different but not necessarily

---

1. Nogalski, "Reading the Book of the Twelve Theologically," 115–16.

2. Nogalski, "Reading the Book of the Twelve Theologically," 116–17.

3. Nogalski, "Reading the Book of the Twelve Theologically," 118.

adjacent prophetic writings," and "allusions to other texts both inside and outside the Book of the Twelve."[4]

Paul R. House's monograph *The Unity of the Twelve* (1990) seeks to understand the large-scale meaning of the Twelve in its final, canonical form.[5] Regarding the structure of the Twelve, he sees Hosea through Micah as expositing the seriousness of "Sin: Covenant and Cosmic," Nahum through Zephaniah as detailing "Punishment: Covenant and Cosmic," and Haggai through Malachi as addressing "Restoration: Covenant and Cosmic."[6] Regarding the plot of the Twelve, House argues for a "U-shaped comic framework"[7] that moves toward a crisis point at the midpoint (Habakkuk), and then rises towards "resolution"[8] in Malachi. Regarding characterization in the Twelve, the main figures are Yhwh, Israel, the nations, and the prophets. Although Yhwh is sovereign, Israel and the nations are continuously at odds, and the prophets have varying relationships to the other parties, House notes that these characters are never stagnant but always "react to the ebb and flow of the plot."[9]

Jason T. LeCureux's monograph *The Thematic Unity of the Book of the Twelve* (2012) argues that the concept of divine and human "returning" (based on the Hebrew word *shuv*) is the core theme that holds the Twelve together.[10] Occurrences of this word are particularly strong at the beginning and end of the Twelve. Thus, Hosea threatens return to Egypt as a punishment (Hos 8:13) and condemns

4. Nogalski, "Reading the Book of the Twelve Theologically," 119.

5. House, *Unity of the Twelve*, 30.

6. House, *Unity of the Twelve*, 72.

7. House, *Unity of the Twelve*, 123.

8. House, *Unity of the Twelve*, 123.

9. House, *Unity of the Twelve*, 219.

10. LeCureux, *Thematic Unity*, 234.

the people as being unwilling to return to Yhwh (Hos 5:4), while still promising a future time of restoration when the Israelites will return (Hos 3:5).[11] Meanwhile, in the midst of a discouraging time in the post-exilic period, Malachi still promises the people that Yhwh will return to them if they will return to him (Mal 3:5).[12] This "returning" to Yhwh includes a return to the important institutions of "the land, Zion, the law, social justice, and the cult," but above all the relationship with Yhwh is primary.[13]

In 2000, James Nogalski and Mavin A. Sweeney assembled an edited volume titled *Reading and Hearing the Book of the Twelve*.[14] It contains one chapter by Paul House, which summarized some arguments similar to those he put forward in his monograph, which we discussed above.[15] Also relevant are the chapters by Rolf Rendtorff and Kenneth Cuffey. Rendtorff's chapter argues that the Day of Yhwh and the nations' repentance are the unifying concepts in the Twelve, while Cuffey's works outward from the remnant promises in Micah to observe relevant connections throughout the Twelve.

Another significant chapter in this volume is John D. W. Watts, "A Frame for the Book of the Twelve: Hosea 1–3 and Malachi."[16] Watts observes that Hos 1–3 and Malachi seem to mirror one another by invoking the theme of God's love for Israel. This can be seen by comparing Hos 3:1 ("The Lord said to me again, 'Go, love a woman who has a lover and is an adulteress, just as the Lord loves the people of Israel . . .'") with Mal 1:2 ("I have loved you,

11. LeCureux, *Thematic Unity*, 236.
12. LeCureux, *Thematic Unity*, 239.
13. LeCureux, *Thematic Unity*, 239.
14. Nogalski and Sweeney, eds., *Reading and Hearing*.
15. House, "Character of God," 125–45.
16. Watts, "Frame," 209–18.

says the Lord. But you say, 'How have you loved us?' Is not Esau Jacob's brother? says the Lord. Yet I have loved Jacob . . .").[17] Therefore, this theme of Israel as ungrateful children encompasses the Twelve as a whole.[18] Meanwhile, Malachi looks to Yhwh's unchanging character (3:6) as the basis of hope for the future. Unlike earlier writings in the Twelve which pronounced judgment for entire generations (see Hos 3:4–5), Mal 3:18 promises that Yhwh in his faithfulness will distinguish between the righteous and the wicked and bless the former.[19]

While the scholars above look for a "main point" that holds the Twelve together, other scholars remain unconvinced. The next section will review proposals for themes that are present within the Twelve, but do not necessarily bear the weight of holding the Twelve together on their own.

THEOLOGICAL ELEMENTS THAT LEND CONTINUITY TO THE TWELVE

Readers of the Twelve will invariably note the multitude of themes that recur throughout. Many scholars who have written on these themes have sought to articulate their unique witnesses without considering other themes to be subordinate or less important. In other words, it is possible to study a certain theme without raising the question of whether or not it serves as the center of the Twelve.

James Nogalski's short essay "Recurring Themes in the Book of the Twelve" (2007) helpfully summarizes the main contours of the Day of Yhwh, the fertility of the land, the fate of God's people, and theodicy.[20] He argues that the

17. Watts, "Frame," 211–12.
18. Watts, "Frame," 213–14.
19. Watts, "Frame," 217.
20. Nogalski, "Recurring Themes," 125–36.

Day of Yhwh is not a single, stable concept[21] and that "the target, the time frame, and the means"[22] can vary significantly in its different instantiations. The fertility of the land emerges as a theme in cases where Yhwh withholds agricultural prosperity to get the peoples' attention, and it also is a means of blessing the people when they repent.[23] The fate of God's people unfolds through increasing warnings of judgment until restoration occurs in the post-exilic books[24] and it involves distinctions between the northern and southern kingdoms[25] and the use of other nations to execute this judgment.[26] The question of theodicy involves the multiple allusions to Exod 34:6–7, as Yhwh's compassion appears to clash with his capacity to execute punishment to Israel and the nations.[27] The end of Malachi develops this theme by noting that Yhwh will deal differently with the righteous and wicked within Israel.[28]

Heath A. Thomas's 2012 essay "Hearing the Minor Prophets: The Book of the Twelve and God's Address" succinctly summarizes a number of concerns and topics relevant to the theological interpretation of the Twelve. He begins with the familiar introductory questions of the relevance of the historical prophets for reading the books[29] and whether and how the individual books should be read as part of the larger canonical collection of the Twelve.[30]

21. Nogalski, "Recurring Themes," 125.
22. Nogalski, "Recurring Themes," 126.
23. Nogalski, "Recurring Themes," 128–29.
24. Nogalski, "Recurring Themes," 130.
25. Nogalski, "Recurring Themes," 131.
26. Nogalski, "Recurring Themes," 132.
27. Nogalski, "Recurring Themes," 132.
28. Nogalski, "Recurring Themes," 134–35.
29. Thomas, "Hearing the Minor Prophets," 357–59.
30. Thomas, "Hearing the Minor Prophets," 359–63.

Thomas then briefly exposits four key theological themes in the Twelve: "history and theodicy" (note that theodicy was one of the major themes covered in the Nogalski article summarized above), "Israel and the nations," "future hope," and "life before God."[31] As an example of his findings, the final category here of "life before God" involves three main points: "cultivating wisdom," "repenting," and "waiting on God in perseverance."[32] For "cultivating wisdom," Thomas points to Hos 14:9, stating,

> The 'wise' reader will attend to the ways of God demonstrated in the history of theology of the Twelve. The past sin of God's people as well as future hope in God's restoration serve as a frame within which the wise reader can orient his or her life. History is not meaningless but anticipates God's restoration in Zion through his justice with Israel and the nations. Wisdom is recognizing and embracing God's ways.[33]

Next, Thomas adopts a broader vantage point and examines the function and message of the Twelve within the Christian Bible as a whole, a discussion he groups under the headings of "The Story of Israel, the Story of Jesus," "The Once and Future King," "Jesus, Judgment, and Salvation," and "Life under the Son."[34]

While, as noted above, there are many themes that run throughout the Twelve, other issues emerge in discrete parts of this corpus. In the next section, we will turn our attention to studies that examine theological topics in particular parts of the Twelve.

---

31. Thomas, "Hearing the Minor Prophets," 363–71.
32. Thomas, "Hearing the Minor Prophets," 369.
33. Thomas, "Hearing the Minor Prophets," 369.
34. Thomas, "Hearing the Minor Prophets," 372–78.

SPECIFIC THEOLOGICAL TOPICS IN THE BOOK OF THE TWELVE

When we move to an even more "micro" level of study, we find a number of theological motifs that appear throughout the Twelve. Yet some theological motifs are restricted to just a couple of books. Many scholars have discovered valuable insights by focusing on these "minor" themes or by looking at smaller subsections of the Twelve.

In 2015, Mark J. Boda et al. released an edited volume titled *The Book of the Twelve and the New Form Criticism*.[35] Although its particular focus is on the methodology of new form criticism, several of the essays, such as those by Beth Stovell, Marvin Sweeney, and Mark Boda, explore the theological insights made possible by this method.

Beth M. Stovell's "I Will Make Her Like a Desert" looks at feminine and agricultural imagery (similar to the theme of fertility discussed in Nogalski's article mentioned above) in Hosea and Micah. She particularly focuses on how Micah makes references to Hosea, examining how metaphors and genres interact to create new meanings in new contexts.[36] For example, Hos 9:11-14 uses the metaphor of infertility to describe judgment on Israel, progressing from "no birth, no pregnancy, no conception" (9:11) to child sacrifice (9:13), and ultimately bodies incapable of conception (9:14).[37] In contrast, while Mic 4:9-10 likewise uses childbirth imagery, Micah's purpose is to use this imagery in hopeful ways that describe restoration. To do this, Micah draws in the Daughter Zion tradition not found in Hosea.[38]

---

35. Boda et al., eds., *Book of the Twelve*.
36. Stovell, "I Will Make Her Like a Desert," 48.
37. Stovell, "I Will Make Her Like a Desert," 53-54.
38. Stovell, "I Will Make Her Like a Desert," 54-55.

Marvin Sweeney's "Form and Eschatology" begins with the observation that the Hebrew and Greek canonical orders of the Twelve are different,[39] and that each of the individual prophetic books has its own perspective on future expectations.[40] In this way, Sweeney's study is similar to Thomas' as it focuses on the category of future hope, yet Sweeney narrows his focus giving Hosea, Micah, and Malachi as examples. Hosea calls for a return to the old united monarchy (Hos 3:4–5) rather than the often apostate northern kingdom and its policy of foreign alliances (14:3 [14:4 MT]),[41] while Micah anticipates Jerusalem's destruction (Mic 3:12),[42] followed by the rise of the ruler (5:2 [5:1 MT]) who will rescue them from the Assyrians (5:6 [5:5 MT]).[43] Finally, at the very end of the Twelve, Malachi looks forward to the restoration of the temple on the Day of the LORD (Mal 3:3–4), with the sending of Elijah (4:5–6 [3:23–24 MT]) to bring this day to pass.[44]

Mark Boda's "A Deafening Call to Silence" surveys places throughout the Twelve where human voices directly or indirectly speak to YHWH.[45] He finds that all of the first eight books (Hosea through Habakkuk), with the exceptions of Obadiah and Nahum, contain various prayers to YHWH. For example, in Hos 2:23 [2:25 MT] the people are depicted as saying "You are my God" in a time of future restoration,[46] an expression echoed by YHWH in 8:2 when the people attempt to cry "My God, we—Israel—know you!" even

39. Sweeney, "Form and Eschatology," 140–41.
40. Sweeney, "Form and Eschatology," 142.
41. Sweeney, "Form and Eschatology," 144–45.
42. Sweeney, "Form and Eschatology," 150.
43. Sweeney, "Form and Eschatology," 151.
44. Sweeney, "Form and Eschatology," 158.
45. Boda, "Call to Silence," 184.
46. Boda, "Call to Silence," 185.

though they are walking in disobedience.⁴⁷ Significantly, after Habakkuk the human address to Yhwh disappears and is replaced by three commands to be silent before Yhwh (Hab 2:20; Zeph 1:7; Zech 2:13 [2:17 MT]).⁴⁸ Surprisingly, prayer to Yhwh does not resume in the post-exilic books usually associated with the theme of "restoration,"⁴⁹ as other clues in this portion of the Twelve suggest that true repentance must be demonstrated first.⁵⁰

In 2003, Paul L. Redditt and Aaron Schart released an edited volume titled *Thematic Threads in the Book of the Twelve*,⁵¹ with essays divided into the separate sections of "Method," "Canonical Order," and "Thematic Threads." Essays like those by De Vries and Albertz provide significant theological readings of themes that are part of the Twelve.

Simon J. De Vries, in "Futurism in the Preexilic Minor Prophets Compared with That of the Postexilic Minor Prophets,"⁵² looks at the use of temporal particles (then, now, afterwards, etc.)⁵³ throughout the Twelve, noting whether they are original or later insertions in each case. For example, in Hos 5:7b ("*Now* the new moon shall devour them along with their fields") the phrase is original, whereas in Hos 1:5 ("*On that day* I will break the bow of Israel in the valley of Jezreel") is redactional.⁵⁴ After synthesizing his results across the full corpus, he notes general tendencies of how temporal particles are used differently in the preexilic and postexilic books. He points to the implications of

47. Boda, "Call to Silence," 185.
48. Boda, "Call to Silence," 201.
49. Boda, "Call to Silence," 203.
50. Boda, "Call to Silence," 203.
51. Redditt and Schart, eds., *Thematic Threads*.
52. De Vries, "Futurism," 252–72.
53. De Vries, "Futurism," 252.
54. De Vries, "Futurism," 253–54.

these observations for themes of judgment and salvation in each section of the preexilic and postexilic prophets in the Twelve. In this, De Vries shares an interest in future expectations with Thomas and Sweeney.

Rainer Albertz, in "Exile as Purification: Reconstructing the 'Book of the Four'"[55] mixes together questions about redaction and theology. He starts by observing the similar superscriptions found in Hosea, Amos, Micah, and Zephaniah, noting that this serves to unify their message and draw comparison between the judgments on Israel and Judah.[56] Furthermore, he notes a significant theological theme inserted by a redactor that binds the four books together: "We have one purification passage at the end of each of the four books (Hos 14:2–4; Amos 9:7–10; Mic 5:9–13; Zeph 3:11–13), and one additional purification passage in the beginning of the first and of the last book each (Hos 3:1–5; Zeph 1:4–6)."[57] Albertz concludes by arguing that the editor who joined these four books together believed that the institutions of the pre-exilic period (such as the kingship, etc.) were inherently corrupt and had to be removed in order for the people to be made right.[58]

Besides De Vries and Albertz, other essays in *Thematic Threads in the Book of the Twelve* explore specific theological themes in the Twelve. While James Crenshaw's essay explores theodicy in the Twelve, which we will explore in more detail in chapter 7 of this book, James Nogalski explores the day of Yhwh in the Book of the Twelve (discussed in our chapter 5).[59] Stephen Tuell compares the

55. Albertz, "Exile," 232–51.
56. Albertz, "Exile," 237.
57. Albertz, "Exile," 240.
58. Albertz, "Exile," 250.
59. Crenshaw, "Theodicy," 175–91; Nogalski, "Day(s) of YHWH," 192–213.

theology of the prophecies of Haggai and Zechariah with Ezekiel, while Burkard Zapff points to the picture of the nations in Micah in comparison to the rest of the Twelve.[60] House studies the theological implications of the calls for repentance throughout the Twelve, which we will explore further in chapter 4.[61]

In 2008, Mark Boda and Michael Floyd released an edited volume titled *Tradition in Transition: Haggai and Zechariah 1–8 in the Trajectory of Hebrew Theology*.[62] Although this work focuses chiefly on one portion of the Twelve, a number of its essays, like Paul Redditt's, have either a relevant theological focus or integrate their results into larger sections of the canon.

Paul L. Redditt's "The King in Haggai—Zechariah 1–8 and the Book of the Twelve" begins with the observation that the positive treatment of Zerubbabel as the ruler who might resume the Davidic kingship in Haggai and Zech 1–8 is a far more optimistic treatment of the idea of monarchy than what is found elsewhere in the Twelve.[63] Redditt's case is:

> (1) that Hosea, Amos, Micah, and Zephaniah, individually and as a Book of the Four, typically viewed individual kings negatively, anticipating their punishment; (2) that Hos 3:5ab plus 1:7 and 11, Amos 9:11–15, most of Mic 4–5 (though not 4:9–10) and possibly 2:12–13, and perhaps Zeph 3:14–20—with its emphasis on the kingship of Yhwh—as well as possibly Zech 9:1–10 may be seen as additions bringing about an early

---

60. Tuell, "Haggai–Zechariah," 273–91; Zapff, "Perspective on the Nations," 292–312.

61. House, "Endings as New Beginnings," 313–38.

62. Boda and Floyd, eds., *Tradition in Transition*.

63. Redditt, "King," 56.

Persian period "pro-Davidic recension" of the developing Book of the Twelve in sympathy with Hag 2:20–23 and Zech 4:6–10a, and 6:12; and (3) that the redactor of Zech 9–14 tempers that optimism with criticism of the Davidides. In the process, it will become clear that a focus on the king offers a surprisingly good avenue into discerning aspects of the growth of the Twelve.[64]

Redditt's essay is a good example of the intertwining of redactional and theological questions, as it isolates different viewpoints towards kingship over time and identifies these ideologies with different diachronic strata within the Twelve. Based on these results, Redditt argues that parts of the "Book of the Four" (Hosea, Amos, Micah, Zephaniah)—books some have deemed the earliest books of the Twelve—are actually later than the books written after the Babylonian exile (post-exilic) and are responding to them.[65] Redditt further argues that the period of "pro-Davidic" optimism peaked around 500 BCE, with the unclear references to the "Branch" in Zech 3:8, 10 marking a time when hopes for Zerubbabel had faded.[66]

Besides Redditt's essay, other essays in *Tradition in Transition* are relevant for the theological interpretation of the Twelve. Lena-Sofia Tiemeyer's chapter explores the horses and riders of Zech 1–6 with the cherubim of Ezekiel.[67] Dominic Rudman compares the figure of Satan in Zech 3 with its occurrences in Job 1–2 and 1 Chr 21,[68] and

64. Redditt, "King," 56–57.
65. Redditt, "King," 81.
66. Redditt, "King," 82.
67. Tiemeyer, "Zechariah's Spies," 104–27.
68. Rudman, "Zechariah and the Satan Tradition," 191–209.

Holger Delkurt studies the themes of guilt and forgiveness in Zech 1–6.[69]

In 2012, Rainer Albertz et al. released an edited volume entitled *Perspectives on the Formation of the Book of the Twelve*.[70] Although, as the title implies, its interests were chiefly on the formation of the Twelve, several of the essays explored theological themes as part of their investigations. The essays are divided into the sections of "Methodological Issues," "Editorial Issues," "Historical Issues," and "Issues Concerning the Canon." Many of the essays in the "Editorial Issues" section explore the integration of individual books (or sub-collections of books) within the Twelve. Of these essays, two have a thematic focus: Mark Biddle examines the kingship and Zion traditions in Mic 4–5 and the rest of the Twelve,[71] similar to elements of Redditt's study of kingship and Judith Gärtner discusses Jerusalem's role as both the center of Israel's cult and as an eschatological gathering point for the nations in Zeph 3.[72]

In 2020, Lena-Sofia Tiemeyer and Jakob Wöhrle released an edited volume titled *The Book of the Twelve: Composition, Reception, and Interpretation*.[73] The essays in this work are divided into four sections: "General Topics," "Issues in Interpretation," "Textual Transmission and Reception History," and "The Theology of the Book of the Twelve." While the fourth section focuses most extensively on theological aspects of the Twelve, the essays in the "General Topics" section engage the question of the history of composition of the Twelve, which often examine theological unity as part of this discussion. The

---

69. Delkurt, "Sin and Atonement," 235–51.

70. Albertz et al., eds., *Perspectives on the Formation*.

71. Biddle, "Dominion Comes to Jerusalem," 253–68.

72. Gärtner, "Jerusalem," 269–83.

73. Tiemeyer and Wöhrle, eds., *The Book of the Twelve*.

third section "Issues in Interpretation" includes a chapter by Craig A. Evans, "The Book of the Twelve in Jesus and the New Testament,"[74] which addresses many questions that would be relevant for the reading of the Twelve from a Christian perspective. Finally, the six chapters in the fourth section ("The Theology of the Book of the Twelve") address the theological themes in the Twelve of "Judgment and Grace," "Kingship," "Geography," "First Fruits Rites," The Nations," and "Exile," respectively.

VIEWING THE BIG PICTURE

What general trends are observable regarding the different types of theological approaches that have been applied to the Book of the Twelve? Many different answers have been given to similar questions. In the case of the debate over whether or not there is a central theme (or narrative) in the Twelve, the sources covered in this chapter approached this issue by (1) looking for a theme that is persistently present throughout; (2) looking for a theme that appears at (or near) the beginning and end of the Twelve; or (3) finding a "parade" of themes as one proceeds in a linear direction. Likewise, in the brief survey of different subthemes found throughout the Twelve, three recurring topics were creation, kingship, and future expectations. The investigations in the following chapters will further develop more of the discussions around these issues.

CONCLUSION

In this chapter, we have explored the various theological approaches to the Twelve from 1990 through 2020.

---

74. Evans, "The Book of the Twelve in Jesus and the New Testament," 385–414.

Examining these studies has shown us that scholars have asked many different theological questions of the Twelve. Some scholars think there is a central unifying theme for the Twelve as a whole, while others are more interested in how multiple minor themes coexist and relate to one another. Chapters 3–7 of this book will provide more in-depth treatments of some of these themes, starting in chapter 3 with the issue of the Davidic kingship, and whether or not it will return in the future.

REFLECTION QUESTIONS:

1. What are the three different approaches to exploring the theology of the Book of the Twelve discussed in this chapter?

2. Which of the theological topics covered in the chapter did you find compelling or interesting? Why?

3. What lingering questions does exploring the theology of the Twelve raise for you? Why?

3

RESTORATION OF THE DAVIDIC MONARCHY

INTRODUCTION

WHILE TODAY, IN MOST ways those in the British monarchy are viewed more as figureheads than as the ultimate sovereign rulers, the ancient world had its own hopes and expectations for its kings. These hopes and expectations form a theme throughout the Twelve. This theme is built on the hopes surrounding King David's family line and the expectations for a future king who will rule the nations from Jerusalem. Yet these hopes are also understood alongside the vision of YHWH as the ultimate king.

While we can identify the theme itself, what it means and how it develops across the Twelve is not as straightforward. Scholars debate the precise way that this important theme emerges in the Twelve. In order to better understand it, in this chapter, we will look not only at direct references to David or his house/line, but also to all activities that could be related to him: ruling, administering justice, fighting on behalf of his people, conquering the nations, and even participating in priestly rituals.

To understand how David and his house relate to the Old Testament overall, we begin this chapter with a brief survey of kingship in the Old Testament and in the areas surrounding Israel in the ancient Near East. We will then move through the Book of the Twelve, focusing on key texts around Davidic kingship, giving particular attention to Hosea, Amos, Micah, Haggai, and Zechariah. As the chapter concludes, we will talk about how these different pictures of kingship give us more insight into the themes of David's family line (his house) and about kingship more broadly in the Twelve.

KINGSHIP IN THE ANCIENT NEAR EAST AND THE OLD TESTAMENT

To understand David's specific form of kingship and the expectations associated with it, it is helpful to zoom out our camera to a big picture view of what kingship was like in the ancient world. The cultures that surrounded the early Israelites impacted what they thought about their kings. For this reason, we will discuss not only kingship as we see it pictured in the Old Testament, but also in the perspectives of Israel's ancient Near Eastern next-door neighbors.

The vast majority of ancient Near Eastern societies were ruled by monarchies. Kings were always understood to be closely related to the gods, but this was understood in diverse ways in different places and times.[1] For example, the Egyptians generally viewed their kings as being outrightly divine, while the Assyrians and Babylonians instead

1. Fox, "Kingship," 475.

saw their kings as acting as representatives of certain chief gods,[2] or possibly as (in the case of portions of Assyrian history) "an earthly instance of the power of the national god."[3] Acting in this capacity, ancient Near Eastern kings were expected to maintain justice in keeping with the will of their gods, lead their people in battle against their enemies,[4] and make sure their temples were in good condition and well-supplied with offerings.[5]

Israel was unique in its cultural environment because it did not have a king during the earliest phases of its existence. Instead, during those early times, Yhwh alone was Israel's king. The Psalms describe Yhwh the king as like a warrior who had victory over the natural world (Ps 29:10). His universal kingship over all creation was based on his role as creator of all things (Ps 96:10).[6] Because Yhwh was considered the great king over all things, while in principle there was nothing wrong with Israel having a king (Deut 17:14–20), Israel's initial request for a human king was considered an act of faithlessness and rebellion (1 Sam 8:4–8). Yet God was gracious to Israel anyway. He chose to give them the human king they requested, despite their problematic reasons for wanting one.

In the aftermath of the tragedy that was Israel's first king, Saul, God revealed through David what the ideal king should look like. First, he must be a man after God's own heart (1 Sam 13:14), acting as someone who trusts Yhwh and seeks his will. Second, he must acknowledge Yhwh's ultimate kingship. We see this in David when he brought the ark of Yhwh into Jerusalem in 2 Sam 6:1–15,

2. Boadt, *Reading the Old Testament*, 207.
3. Jones, "Divine and Non-Divine Kingship," 244.
4. Boadt, *Reading the Old Testament*, 207.
5. Fox, "Kingship," 476.
6. Flynn, *Yhwh Is King*, 175.

an act that symbolically demonstrated David's submission to Yhwh's sovereignty. Third, he must rule his people in a way that upholds justice, as David did in 2 Sam 8:15. Finally, he must be a mighty warrior, as we see in the numerous narratives of David in combat.[7]

Significantly, in the formal covenant Yhwh makes with David, Yhwh establishes several attributes about his role as king. First, although David will not build Yhwh's temple, David's son will (2 Sam 7:5–7, 13). Second, Yhwh will make David's name great (v. 9), with a "house" (v. 11) and kingdom that will last forever (v. 16). Third, Israel will have its own land and be safe from its enemies (vv. 10–11). Finally, David's son, the one to build Yhwh's temple, will be like a son to Yhwh (v. 14) and will always experience Yhwh's "steadfast love" (v. 15). These expectations—both concerning God's gracious initiative and the human king's responsibilities—set the reader's expectations through the narratives of the united and divided monarchies that follow. Thus, through the books of 1 and 2 Kings, the kings who are praised are those who are faithful in establishing justice, taking care of the temple, and staying away from idolatry.[8]

But Israel's views of kingship itself and God's promises of kingship were about to be tested. After Israel's monarchy divided to form two kingdoms, Israel to the north and Judah to the south, the empires of Assyria and then Babylon took over and devastated the Israelite kingship. In 722 BCE, Assyria largely destroyed the northern kingdom of Israel. This left behind a severely weakened and small southern kingdom of Judah, the kingdom where Jerusalem sat as capital city and as the holy place of God's temple. After many rounds of violence and invasion, in 586 BCE, the Babylonians sacked the city of Jerusalem

7. Abernethy and Goswell, *God's Messiah*, 56–60.

8. Abernethy and Goswell, *God's Messiah*, 83.

and destroyed the first Jerusalem temple. In the face of this horrific defeat, the Israelites began to question what this meant for Israelite kingship. Had the promises of God's devotion not only to David but to all of his generations of descendants been meaningless?

These questions of kingship are all over the Psalms. When we view the Psalms not as a collection of songs or poems, but as a book composed to respond to the situations of its time, we can see this experience of kingship impacting its arrangement. The first three books have a number of psalms in which the Davidic king serves Yhwh and is a messianic figure (see Pss 2, 41, 72).[9] However, a crucial shift occurs in Pss 89–90, as 89:49 [89:50 MT] questions the present existence of Yhwh's past love for David, and immediately Ps 90:1–2 expresses immediate reliance on Yhwh's protection alone.[10] The remaining content of the Psalter likewise moves "away from hopes centering on the Davidic royal house toward an exclusive reliance on Yhwh as king."[11] We see a similar shift of emphasis from human to divine kingship when we compare 1–2 Chronicles with Samuel–Kings.[12] Like the Psalms, the Book of the Twelve covers a broad swath of time. The prophets of the Twelve's earliest books originate in the time before the devastation of the Davidic monarchy by the Babylonians. Other prophets in the Twelve date to a time when Persian rulers took over the spaces where Babylon had ruled and the Israelite people were allowed to return to their land. Not surprisingly, the Twelve reflects many of the shifts we find elsewhere in the Old Testament around the hopes of David's line and the tension around future kingship.

9. Abernethy and Goswell, *God's Messiah*, 183–85.
10. Abernethy and Goswell, *God's Messiah*, 185.
11. Abernethy and Goswell, *God's Messiah*, 193.
12. Abernethy and Goswell, *God's Messiah*, 210–23.

THE DAVIDIC MONARCHY IN THE BOOK OF THE TWELVE

We see these points of hope and tension when we explore the Book of the Twelve. Here we will focus on Hosea, Amos, Micah, Haggai, and Zechariah, which speak the most obviously about the Davidic monarchy. Before we start examining these books of the Twelve where kingship is present as a theme, it is helpful to take a moment to discuss the books that we omitted. Given that the remaining seven books have no discussion of a future king from the line of David,[13] should that from the outset cast doubt upon this subject being a significant theme in the Twelve? Not necessarily. Each of these other books has a focus on topics that are less connected to Davidic kingship.

While the precise historical setting of Joel is obscure (and its canonical location in the Twelve differs in the Hebrew and Greek collections), Joel describes a future deliverance of Judah accomplished by Yhwh, which contains notable parallels with the beginning and end of Amos (see discussion below).[14] Obadiah and Jonah are entirely concerned with the fate of other nations (Edom and Nineveh).[15] Nahum is narrowly focused on the judgment of Assyria, and Habakkuk likewise deals with Babylon (although stating in Hab 3:13 that Yhwh came to save his people and his anointed one).[16] Zephaniah spends time describing the restoration of Judah, and points to Yhwh as king (3:15). This reference to Yhwh's kingship does not necessarily dismiss the physical descendants of David, but

---

13. Goswell, "David Their King," 226.
14. Sweeney, "Place and Function of Joel," 148, 150–51.
15. Petterson, "Shape of the Davidic Hope," 242.
16. Petterson, "Shape of the Davidic Hope," 242.

leaves the topic unexplored.[17] Malachi promises that YHWH will come after the ministry of a messenger (3:1), an event that readers of the Twelve should associate with the future promises of restoration given elsewhere in this corpus.[18] In this way, each of these books leave room for Davidic kingship as a broader theme in the Twelve without directly proclaiming it in their own pages. Now we will proceed to the parts of the Twelve where Davidic kingship is more obvious as a theme (or at least, there is the possibility of this theme present), beginning with Hosea.

Hosea

Hosea's relationship with kingship is complicated. Hosea frequently criticizes the Israelite kings who reigned during his ministry. In 8:4 he seemingly denies the legitimacy of the entire northern kingdom when he says, "They made kings, but not through me; they set up princes, but without my knowledge." This negative appraisal of the northern kingdom as a whole could be taken as an implicit argument for the necessity of the re-unification of all Israel under a Davidic ruler.[19] However, his strong indictments of the Israelite priests (5:1) and prophets (9:7) of this period show that *all* of the offices of leadership in the north are corrupt, and thus these statements alone are not evidence that Hosea believed that only the Davidic line was legitimate.[20]

The first key text relating to the future of the Davidic Monarchy in Hosea is 1:10–11 [2:1–2 MT]. Hosea envisions the children of Israel as one day being a vast multitude, and being called the "children of the living God" (1:10 [2:1 MT]),

   17. Petterson, "Shape of the Davidic Hope," 242–43.
   18. Petterson, "Shape of the Davidic Hope," 244–45.
   19. Goswell, "David Their King," 218.
   20. Goswell, "David Their King," 219.

in contrast to the prophetic name given earlier to one of his children in 1:9, "Lo-ammi," which means "not my people." Next, in 1:11 [2:2 MT] he promises, "The people of Judah and the people of Israel shall be gathered together, and they shall appoint for themselves one head; and they shall take possession of the land, for great shall be the day of Jezreel." Many readers would intuitively understand this "one head" to be a future king from the line of David.[21] However, some factors would caution against adopting this reading hastily. The word used here for "head" is used for the regional leaders who ruled before David, and never for the Davidic monarchy itself.[22] Also, the references elsewhere in the book to the restoration of the people involve Yhwh himself accomplishing the deliverance (2:23 [2:25 MT], "I will sow him for myself in the land"), not a human king.[23] This king additionally is restricted in scope to the land of Israel and is not said to conquer the nations.[24] Nonetheless, it is still entirely possible that 1:10–11 [2:1–2 MT] expresses hope for a future ruler from the line of David.[25]

The second such key text in Hosea—and indeed the only explicit reference to David in the book—is found in 3:5. After Hosea is commanded to take Gomer back (3:1–3), he declares that there will be an extended period of time where the monarchy and all worship functions will be abolished (3:4). He then states in 3:5 "Afterward the Israelites shall return and seek the Lord their God, and David their king; they shall come in awe to the Lord and to his goodness in the latter days." Unfaithful Israel, like Gomer, will be restored by God. The word used here for

21. Petterson, "Shape of the Davidic Hope," 240.
22. Goswell, "David Their King," 220.
23. Goswell, "David Their King," 221.
24. Goswell, "David Their King," 214.
25. Goswell, "David Their King," 222.

"seek" occurs elsewhere in Hosea regarding the worship of Yhwh (5:16, 15; 7:10).[26] At the very least, Hos 3:5 promises a future time when the Israelites will turn from idolatry, and this revival of correct worship will occur alongside a restoration of the monarchy. While this initially appears to be irrefutable proof of a future for the literal Davidic monarchy,[27] at the same time, "it cannot be said that Hosea places any *emphasis* on a Davidic hope, for this is the only Hosean text that mentions David and the focus is completely on the people's response to Yhwh in the last part of the verse."[28] Weighing Hosea alongside other parts of the Twelve, we might say that, while Hosea may hint at Davidic kingship, Hosea's primary focus is on the picture of Yhwh as king rather than on a human king.

Amos

In addition to having two occurrences of David's name (6:5; 9:11), Amos contains a number of passages that discuss kingship, restoration to Yhwh, and the nations, and this material also plays a role in determining this book's stance on the future of the Davidic monarchy. Although Amos ministered in northern Israel (1:1), he begins his message by locating Yhwh's revelation as coming from Jerusalem (1:2). Many see this beginning in conjunction with the repeated lament that the people did not "return" to Yhwh (see 4:6–11) as pointing to a future in which all Israel will be united under the Davidic monarchy.[29] However, the location of Jerusalem alone does not necessarily carry an association with the Davidic monarchy, and the commands to

26. Goswell, "David Their King," 224.
27. Petterson, "Shape of the Davidic Hope," 240.
28. Goswell, "David Their King," 222.
29. Goswell, "David in the Prophecy," 245.

"seek" Yhwh in 5:4–14 are based around righteous living, not the location for worship.[30]

Furthermore, parallel phrases used in Amos's neighboring books in the Twelve do not encourage a connection between restoration of piety and Davidic rule. The beginning and end of Amos closely mirror key passages addressing restoration in Joel: compare Joel 3:16 [4:16 MT] with Amos 1:2, and Joel 3:18 [4:18 MT] with Amos 9:13. While Joel 3 [4 MT] as a whole describes Yhwh judging the nations and blessing his people, it does not include reference to David. We can also draw parallels between Mic 4:2b ("For out of Zion shall go forth instruction, and the word of the Lord from Jerusalem") and Amos 1:2 (similar to Joel 3:16 [4:16 MT]). Once again, though, Mic 4 as a whole treats Yhwh as the king, not a ruler from David's line.[31]

The first direct reference to David in Amos is found in 6:5, "who sing idle songs to the sound of the harp, and like David improvise on instruments of music." Even a brief glance at the immediate context of this verse (6:4–7) shows that it is a condemnation of the Israelites who feel secure in their luxury rather than seeking Yhwh for protection. Therefore, this only brings up David in his capacity as a worship leader, and in no way should be taken as messianic.[32]

The second, and indeed more significant, reference to David in Amos occurs near the end of the book, at 9:11, "On that day I will raise up the booth of David that is fallen, and repair its breaches, and raise up its ruins, and rebuild it as in the days of old." This verse sits alongside three subsequent promises that "they may possess the remnant of Edom" (v. 12), "I will restore the fortunes of my people Israel" (v. 14), and "they shall never again be

---

30. Goswell, "David in the Prophecy," 246.
31. Goswell, "David in the Prophecy," 246–47.
32. Goswell, "David in the Prophecy," 248–50.

plucked up out of the land that I have given them" (v. 15). Together these expectations certainly seem to claim that a restoration of the Davidic monarchy will be part of the revival of covenant faithfulness and blessing in the future. However, what exactly is this "booth of David" in 9:11? Attention to the underlying Hebrew suggests that it could actually point to the temple. The same word for "booth" is used in Isa 4:6, where Yhwh creates a canopy of cloud by day and smoke and fire by night to protect Zion (Isa 4:4–6), a motif that is obviously reminiscent of the exodus as well as the divine presence in the tabernacle (Exod 40:38).[33] But why is David mentioned? David brought the ark of the Lord into Jerusalem in 2 Sam 6, establishing this city as the center of worship for Yhwh.[34] Amos 9:11 also functions to create a contrast with the condemnation of the false sanctuary of Israel at Bethel in 7:9, 13, with this location again being triggered by the mention of the "altar" in 9:1. Therefore, "The destruction of the false sanctuary at Bethel finds its positive counterpart in the restoration of the Jerusalem sanctuary (9:11)."[35]

However, readers will notice that 9:12 promises possession of the nations. Doesn't this hope shift the focus away from the cult to military conquest? Crucially, the verb is plural rather than singular (*"they* may possess"), and the promise is therefore made to the entire nation rather than to the action of a specific leader. This can be understood as a "democratization of Davidic promises,"[36] the dispersing of these promises among the people. This interpretation is further supported by the recurring use of this concept of communal possession in Obadiah (1:17,

33. Goswell, "David in the Prophecy," 252–53.
34. Goswell, "David in the Prophecy," 254.
35. Goswell, "David in the Prophecy," 256.
36. Goswell, "David in the Prophecy," 257.

19, 20), where promises that were originally made to David are now given to all the people.[37]

Conversely, others have argued that Amos 9:11 does signify a hope for a literal restoration of the Davidic monarchy. Their basis for this is that the "booth of David" is instead a reference to the presently weakened state of the Davidic line as compared to its previous powerful state. Additionally, in v. 12 the ones who are said to possess the remnant of Edom (described as "they") could be identified with the "booth of David," viewing the members of this kingdom collectively.[38] Another relevant point to consider is that the verb used for the "fallen" state of the booth of David in 9:11 also occurs in 5:2 and 8:14. In both cases it means the house of Israel as a whole, not the temple.[39] The promise in 9:11 that Yhwh will "raise" the fallen booth of David is reminiscent of the promise "I will raise up your offspring after you" in 2 Sam 7:12, which is directly addressing the lineage of David.[40] Thus, with his references to kingship and to David, Amos appears to repeatedly extend the promises to David beyond a single royal figure to all of God's people and demonstrate that God himself is the ultimate king. While Amos may offer some hope for a restored Davidic monarchy, he does this with his extended vision ever present.

Micah

The prediction of a future ruler from Bethlehem in Mic 5:1–4 [4:14—5:3 MT] is well-known due to its messianic usage in the New Testament (Matt 2:6). However, in Micah this passage is the third part of a sequence of short descriptions

---

37. Goswell, "David in the Prophecy," 257.
38. Petterson, "Shape of the Davidic Hope," 241.
39. Timmer, *Non-Israelite Nations*, 54.
40. Timmer, *Non-Israelite Nations*, 54.

of distress followed by hope (see the pattern established by Mic 4:9–10, 11–13). When we read this messianic figure in light of the promises of divine rescue and rule over the nations already made in 4:10 and 4:13, this figure seems to be one more picture of hope among many rather than a figure with a giant spotlight upon him. Notably, the messianic figure also disappears after 5:4 [5:3 MT].[41] Several features in 5:2 [5:1 MT] show us that this future ruler is fully "subordinated" to Yhwh. The appellation of "king" is conspicuously withheld from him (in a manner similar to Isa 9:6 and 11:1, both of which are discussing a figure from the line of David). The future ruler will "come forth" for Yhwh, pointing to how he will "serve God's purposes."[42] Instead of using the title "king" for this future figure, Micah reserves the title of "king" for Yhwh himself (see 2:13; 4:7).[43]

But what exactly does this future ruler do? The only role assigned to him is described in 5:4 [5:3 MT] with "And he shall stand and feed his flock in the strength of the Lord." Elsewhere in Micah, it is Yhwh alone that gathers the scattered people (2:12; 4:6), and as a result "any mention of messianic agency in the rescue of God's people is entirely lacking."[44] The future ruler is also absent in the future military conflict immediately described in 5:5 [5:4 MT], as here it is the people who take the initiative.[45] This continues in vv. 7–9 [vv. 6–8 MT], as the "remnant of Jacob" itself dominates the nations through trust in Yhwh alone ("which do not depend upon people or wait for any mortal," v. 7 [v. 6 MT]), and consequently Yhwh's hand is raised in victory over Israel's

---

41. Goswell, "Davidic Rule in the Prophecy of Micah," 155.
42. Goswell, "Davidic Rule in the Prophecy of Micah," 157.
43. Goswell, "Davidic Rule in the Prophecy of Micah," 158.
44. Goswell, "Davidic Rule in the Prophecy of Micah," 158.
45. Goswell, "Davidic Rule in the Prophecy of Micah," 162.

enemies in v. 9 [v. 8 MT] (a motif also invoked in Isa 26:11).[46] As a result, in this reading, while there will be a future leader from the line of David, his duties are narrowly confined to internal matters, with the historic tasks of military conquest now transferred to Yhwh and the people.

There is another way of reading the evidence from Micah, however. One could also start with Mic 4:8, "And you, O tower of the flock, hill of daughter Zion, to you it shall come, the former dominion shall come, the sovereignty of daughter Jerusalem," and find here a promise of a resumption of traditional Judahite kingship. Likewise, the clearly Davidic promise of one coming from Bethlehem (5:2 [5:1 MT]) is for some sufficient evidence alone that the ruler to come will carry out the same roles as David did previously.[47] Thus, in Micah the evidence for Davidic kingship could go either way, but it seems to lean towards a future Davidic ruler whose power has been narrowed while Yhwh's kingship and the role of the people take a greater place.

Haggai

The key passage potentially relevant for the possibility of a future Davidic hope in the book of Haggai is 2:20–23, specifically the promise given in v. 23: "On that day, says the Lord of hosts, I will take you, O Zerubbabel my servant, son of Shealtiel, says the Lord, and make you like a signet ring; for I have chosen you, says the Lord of hosts." Some have interpreted this verse as stating that Zerubbabel is the future Davidic king. The key terms in this verse are "my servant," "signet ring," and being "chosen," but none of these is

---

46. Goswell, "Davidic Rule in the Prophecy of Micah," 164–65.
47. Petterson, "Shape of the Davidic Hope," 242.

Restoration of the Davidic Monarchy

exclusively applied to royalty.[48] Additionally, in Hag 2:22 it is Yhwh that overthrows the nations, not Zerubbabel.[49]

In the reference to the "signet ring," Haggai is likely drawing from Jer 22:24–30 and its judgment on Jehoiakim's son Jehoiachin (here called Coniah). Jeremiah 22:24–25 states that Yhwh would discard Coniah and hand him over to Babylon even if Coniah was Yhwh's "signet ring." In the context of Haggai, this does not mean that Zerubbabel is necessarily the king himself, but rather that he is "instrumental in re-establishing the Davidic line in Jerusalem" by "rebuilding the temple after the disaster of Coniah."[50]

Conversely, others have pointed to ways that 2:20–23 differs from the earlier oracle of 2:6–9 to show that something other than the restoration of the temple is in view. While both passages begin with the initial phrase "I will shake the heavens and the earth," in v. 7 the "shaking" of the nations leads immediately to the temple being filled with wealth, whereas in vv. 22–23 a number of images are compounded to describe the way that nations will be overthrown. These two passages seem to differentiate two respective sets of nations that either obey or disobey Yhwh.[51] If this conquering of the nations (v. 22) logically leads to Zerubbabel being given special prominence (v. 23), then it is entirely plausible that 2:20–23 describes "Yhwh's undisputed reign by means of his Davidic agent."[52] This could be taken even further, such that 2:20–23 is in fact a forecast of "the overthrow of the Persian Empire and the restoration of the Davidic monarchy in the person of Zerubbabel"[53]

48. Goswell, "David Their King," 228.
49. Goswell, "David Their King," 228.
50. Petterson, "Shape of the Davidic Hope," 236.
51. Timmer, *Non-Israelite Nations*, 172.
52. Timmer, *Non-Israelite Nations*, 173.
53. Redditt, "The King in Haggai–Zechariah 1–8," 59.

and the "signet ring" intentionally points to the judgment of Jer 22:24–30 being overturned.[54] One could also posit that the absence of direct references to Zerubbabel as a king was for the purposes of avoiding outright challenges to Darius's kingship.[55] Thus, it is debatable whether Haggai is pointing to a restoration of the Davidic monarchy through Zerubbabel or not. However, whether Zerubbabel is intended to be pictured as the anticipated Davidic king or not, he does serve as Yhwh's agent and an instrument of Yhwh's rule and reign. In Haggai, this theme emphasizes Yhwh's ultimate power over the nations and his ability to restore his people, a message deeply needed as the people continue to experience foreign rule.

Zechariah

The pivotal passage regarding Zechariah's perspective on the future of the Davidic monarchy is Zech 9:9–10:

> Rejoice greatly, O daughter Zion! Shout aloud, O daughter Jerusalem! Lo, your king comes to you; triumphant and victorious is he, humble and riding on a donkey, on a colt, the foal of a donkey. He will cut off the chariot from Ephraim and the war-horse from Jerusalem; and the battle bow shall be cut off, and he shall command peace to the nations; his dominion shall be from sea to sea, and from the River to the ends of the earth.

Many readers are familiar with 9:9 due to its application to Jesus in the Gospel accounts of Jesus's triumphal entry into Jerusalem (Matt 21:5; John 12:15). However, if we want to clarify the identity of this king in the text's original context, we must take the rest of Zechariah into account.

---

54. Athas, "Failure of Davidic Hope," 230.
55. Athas, "Failure of Davidic Hope," 232.

Restoration of the Davidic Monarchy

Some see this text as an impressionistic description of Yhwh *himself* entering Jerusalem in an "end times" scenario. Those who take this view will point to how the entire book of Zechariah again and again focuses on the idea of Yhwh as king, leading his people. Yhwh promises to come and dwell with his people (2:10 [2:14 MT]; 8:3) and both chs. 9 and 14 as a whole describe Yhwh conquering the nations and ruling from the temple in Jerusalem.[56] (It is especially notable that ch. 14 has no references to David.)[57] If we read Zech 9:9–10 with this in mind, we also notice the descriptions of Yhwh's violence against different nations in 9:1–7,[58] followed by the statement in 9:8 from Yhwh: "Then I will encamp at my house as a guard." Read this way, the king of Zech 9:9 is not picturing a human king who will reinstate the Davidic empire. Instead, this "king" pictures Yhwh's dominion over the entire earth.[59]

Some have struggled with understanding the "king" of 9:9 as Yhwh based on the challenging alternations between third-person description (i.e., 9:4, "But now, *the* Lord will strip it of its possessions . . .") and first-person declarations (i.e., 9:7, "*I* will take away its blood from its mouth") in ch. 9. However, "when identifiable, the speaker or the individual spoken about in Zech 9 is only ever God,"[60] so there is no reason to believe that the "king" of 9:9 suddenly introduces another figure.

While it may initially seem unusual for Yhwh to be "riding on a donkey" (9:9), this anthropomorphism is hardly more of a stretch than Yhwh fighting (9:4) or

---

56. Goswell, "A Theocratic Reading of Zechariah 9:9," 8–9.
57. Meyers and Meyers, "Future Fortunes," 220.
58. Compare Amos 1–2.
59. Goswell, "A Theocratic Reading of Zechariah 9:9," 9.
60. Goswell, "A Theocratic Reading of Zechariah 9:9," 11.

encamping (9:8).⁶¹ Also challenging is the description of the king in 9:9 as being "humble," an adjective that is difficult to apply to Yhwh (or a king in general). However, this could be a reference to the common Old Testament trope of humility preceding exaltation, or possibly a means of communicating Yhwh's gracious lowering of himself to come and save his people (compare Pss 18:35 [18:36 MT]; 45:4 [45:5 MT]).⁶² Furthermore, while we might tend to think of riding on a donkey (Zech 9:9) as connected to humility or gentleness, donkeys could be ridden by leaders (Judg 10:4; 12:14) and were even used in Solomon's ascension to throne (1 Kgs 1:33, 38, 44).⁶³

While the book of Zechariah can be read in such a way that Yhwh himself is the future king, this is not the only option. Some interpreters believe that Zechariah does point to a literal future ruler from the line of David, while others see the character of Zerubbabel himself assuming that role (as seen in the discussion of Haggai above). Arguing for this approach requires scholars to bring in other parts of Zechariah.

To argue for Zerubbabel as the anticipated king of Zech 9:9–10, some scholars point to Zerubbabel's status as an "anointed one" in Zech 4. In Zech 4, the prophet Zechariah sees a lampstand with olive trees on either side (4:1–7), and immediately receives assurance from Yhwh that Zerubbabel will complete the temple (4:8–10). Zechariah then asks Yhwh about the identity of two branches of the olive trees, which pour oil through golden pipes (4:11–13), and Yhwh replies that they are "the two anointed ones who stand by the Lord of the whole earth" (4:14). Many have seen these "two anointed ones" as Joshua the priest and

61. Goswell, "A Theocratic Reading of Zechariah 9:9," 13.
62. Goswell, "A Theocratic Reading of Zechariah 9:9," 15–16.
63. Goswell, "A Theocratic Reading of Zechariah 9:9," 16–17.

Restoration of the Davidic Monarchy

Zerubbabel the king, because both priests and kings were anointed for service in Israel.[64] However, a better translation of the underlying Hebrew would be that these figures are supplying oil rather than being anointed.[65] On this basis, it is more plausible to think these "two anointed ones" are Haggai and Zechariah. This view is further supported by the connections between prophecy and the post-exilic building of the temple elsewhere.[66] So this passage is difficult to use as support for there being an expectation of a future Davidic king in Zech 9:9–10.

Another relevant question in Zechariah is the identity of the "branch" in Zech 3. After Yhwh rebukes Satan for accusing Joshua and provides Joshua with clean clothes in ch. 3, Yhwh promises Joshua, "I am going to bring my servant the Branch" (3:8). A few chapters later, Yhwh commands Zechariah to make a crown and put it on Joshua's head (6:11), and to proclaim

> Here is a man whose name is Branch: for he shall branch out in his place, and he shall build the temple of the Lord. It is he that shall build the temple of the Lord; he shall bear royal honor, and shall sit upon his throne and rule. There shall be a priest by his throne, with peaceful understanding between the two of them (6:12–13).

While many readers may intuitively suspect that here Joshua is identified with the branch, back in 3:8 they seemed to be separate individuals. Joshua is a priest rather than a king, and Jer 23:5–6 and 33:15–16 make it clear that this branch is a descendant of David.[67] Another possible option is

64. Athas, "Failure of Davidic Hope," 237–38.
65. Boda, "Oil, Crowns, and Thrones," 71.
66. Petterson, *Behold Your King*, 81.
67. Petterson, *Behold Your King*, 114; Boda, "Oil, Crowns, and Thrones," 68.

Zerubbabel, since he clearly was involved in building the temple, but Zerubbabel did not successfully restore the Davidic line or usher in an era of peace.[68] On this basis, the branch could be a figure who is coming in the future to build the eschatological temple, rather than the temple of Zerubbabel's time.[69] Another way of configuring the evidence would be to view the branch as an office rather than as a specific person. In this way, Zerubbabel could occupy this position, while still not fulfilling the entirety of its destiny.[70] Thus, the "branch" of Zech 3 could point to Zerubbabel as the anticipated future king of Zech 9:9–10 or to a future king who will restore the Davidic line. But neither of these interpretations make it obvious that Zech 9:9–10 is about a future Davidic human king originally.

Zechariah's frequent discussion of Yhwh either replacing or raising up Israel's "shepherds" also impacts how we read Zech 9:9. First, it is important to know that the term "shepherd" was frequently used in the ancient Near East and in other parts of the Old Testament to designate a king or another form of leader.[71] Zechariah 10:3–4 threatens punishment for the shepherds, but promises to raise up victorious leaders from the flock of the house of Judah, using the terms of the "cornerstone," "tent peg," and "battle bow" to describe these leaders. Read in the context of the description of the king of Zech 9:9, this cornerstone could be a future ruler from the house of David.[72] Similarly, the

---

68. Petterson, *Behold Your King*, 115–16.

69. Petterson, *Behold Your King*, 118–19.

70. Athas, "Failure of Davidic Hope," 235–37.

71. In the Old Testament, examples include God as shepherd who is king in Ezek 34. See Stovell, "God Feeds His Sheep with Justice," 79–81. For more on the metaphor of shepherd and kings, see van Hecke, "Conceptual Blending," 215–32.

72. Meyers and Meyers, "Future Fortunes," 212–15; Petterson,

further rebuke of the worthless shepherds in Zech 11 can be taken as a dramatic retelling of Israel's history in which the rejection of the corrupt leaders implies that Yhwh will eventually bring faithful leaders.[73] (Although it should be noted that this passage has also been read as a prediction of the future and as a reflection on current political upheavals.)[74] A third relevant image is the shocking twist in 13:7-8 that Yhwh himself will strike the shepherd and scatter the sheep, an act that leads to their eventual purification (13:9). While some would naturally see this shepherd as being one of the ruffians condemned in chs. 10-11, an association of this figure with the coming king of 9:9 is plausible in light of the function of the one who is pierced (12:10, see below).[75]

Last but not least, there is a sequence of references to the "house of David" in 12:7, 8 (twice), 10, 12. The passage begins in 12:7-9 with promises of military victory for Judah, but shifts moods to grieving in 12:10 onwards, as the Judahites mourn for the one they have pierced. It is difficult to determine whether this should be related to political challenges of Judah living under Persian rule (a potential case being that the Persians removed one of the Judean governors), or whether it is entirely eschatological.[76] Regardless of exactly who this was intended to picture in Zechariah's time, it is clear that this "house of David" is not the powerful ruling house it was in the past. Zechariah 12:7 makes it clear that the glory of the house of David will not overshadow that of Judah as a whole, and 12:8 states that everyone in Jerusalem will be like David; in other words,

---

Behold Your King, 167.

73. Petterson, *Behold Your King*, 194.
74. Petterson, "Shape of the Davidic Hope," 229-31.
75. Petterson, *Behold Your King*, 211.
76. Meyers and Meyers, "Future Fortunes," 215-16.

there is a movement towards "democratization."⁷⁷ The crucial issue in this passage is of course the identity of "the one they have pierced" in 12:10. If it is a prophet, then the main point could be that the mourning of the house of David represents the royal line sincerely repenting for its long history of ignoring and persecuting the prophets.⁷⁸ Alternatively, the pierced one could be the Davidic king himself. In his suffering he acts like a priest (as in the association of these offices in 3:9), a point reinforced by the presence of priestly families among the mourners.⁷⁹

Because of this complexity, some have argued that Zechariah is full of Davidic kingship imagery, while others have pointed to the centrality of Yhwh's kingship (arguing for the "king" of Zech 9:9–10 as Yhwh himself) and the democratization of the Davidic promises. Zechariah's critiques of the "shepherd" leaders of his time points to the hope that God will restore faithful leaders, but this hope sits under the central picture of Yhwh's role as the ultimate shepherd-king who has dominion over the whole earth.

VIEWING THE BIG PICTURE

While we can see above that there are multiple ways of interpreting the relevant passages about kingship across the Twelve, nonetheless the Twelve does provide specific contours about the theme of Davidic kingship and Yhwh's kingship. Hosea 1:10–11 [2:1–2 MT] promises a future gathering of all the peoples of Israel under one head, and 3:5 states that the people will return to David their king. Amos 9:11 speaks of the restoration of the booth of David. Micah 5:1–4 [4:14—5:3 MT] speaks of a ruler coming

---

77. Meyers and Meyers, "Future Fortunes," 217–18.
78. Meyers and Meyers, "Future Fortunes," 218–19.
79. Petterson, *Behold Your King*, 244–45.

from Bethlehem who will feed his flock. Haggai 2:20–23 promises that Zerubbabel will be Yhwh's signet ring. In Zech 9:9 a king comes riding on a donkey into Jerusalem, which can be connected to the military leaders raised up in 10:4, but can also be seen as emphasizing Yhwh's kingship. Zechariah 12:10–14 provides a final explicit reference to the Davidic house, where all of Jerusalem has the same honor as the house of David, and then the house of David grieves as it mourns for the one that it pierced. These shifting pictures of Davidic kingship and Davidic promises throughout the Twelve supports the claim that in the Twelve the language once used for the human king is replaced largely by language about Yhwh as king.[80] While the Twelve consistently hopes for future faithful leaders who will be part of the Davidic line, the ultimate hope is placed in Yhwh's hands as the supreme king of all creation and extends beyond the human king himself to all of God's people. In making this shift, the Twelve also bears a powerful witness to the love of Yhwh for his people and his desire to gather them to dwell with them.

REFLECTION QUESTIONS:

1. How did the Twelve depict kingship in different ways? Which depictions did you find compelling? Why?

2. The Twelve describes the hope for faithful leaders who are directed by God. What qualities of faithful leaders in the time of the Twelve remain valuable for leaders today? Why?

3. How does the Twelve represent a tension between human kingship and God's kingship? In what way is the picture of God as king still relevant today?

80. Nogalski, "Recurring Themes," 131.

4

REPENTANCE AND RETURN

INTRODUCTION

IN THE PREVIOUS CHAPTER, we explored the theme of the restoration of the Davidic monarchy throughout the Book of the Twelve. In this chapter, we will explore two interrelated themes that are even more prevalent in the Twelve than Davidic monarchy: the themes of repentance and return.

The entire story of the Bible echoes with God's call to repent and return to him. From God's voice in the Garden of Eden asking Adam and Eve where they are hiding after they ate the fruit from the Tree of the Knowledge of Good and Evil (Gen 3:9) to the calls for God's people to come out of sinful Babylon in the book of Revelation (Rev 18:4), the Bible shows us from beginning to end God's repeated desire to draw his people back to himself.

This theme is also core to the Twelve. Key to the story of the Book of the Twelve is the movement back and forth as YHWH and Israel turn away from one another and then turn towards one another, again and again. Yнwн repeatedly calls for the people to repent from their sins and turn back to him so they can once again experience Yнwн's covenant blessings. As we will see, as we read through the Twelve in order, there is an overall purposeful progression from announcements of Israel's guilt, to the people experiencing their deserved punishment, and finally to repentance and restoration.[1] While many scholars see this overarching theme as essential to the organization and purpose of the Twelve, there are nonetheless different interpretations of how each of these sections of the Twelve might be understood. In this chapter, we will trace the development of these themes of repentance and return across the Twelve by following the order of the books within the Twelve.[2]

HOSEA

As the first book in the Twelve, Hosea functions as an introduction, and it sets up the importance of repenting and returning by making the concept of "turning/returning" particularly prominent throughout. Indeed, the Hebrew verb for "turning" or "returning" (*shuv*) occurs twenty-two times in Hosea (some scholars argue there are even one or two more).[3] The very first line of Hosea's prophecy indicates the dire need for repentance by ordering the prophet Hosea to marry an unfaithful wife to mirror the spiritual adultery of the land, which has been unfaithful to the LORD

1. House, *Unity of the Twelve*, 109.

2. As noted in chapter 1 of this book, there are multiple canonical orders of the Twelve, most notably the orders of the MT and the Septuagint. Although there are intriguing differences of significance in the Septuagint ordering of the Twelve, this book chooses to restrict its focus to the ordering of the Twelve used in the Hebrew (and subsequently English) canons.

3. Bowman, "Reading the Twelve as One," 55.

(1:2).[4] Soon afterwards, Israel is called to repent. In the book of Hosea, the nation of Israel is symbolically represented as an adulterous wife: "Plead with your mother, plead—for she is not my wife, and I am not her husband—that she put away her whoring from her face, and her adultery from between her breasts" (2:2 [4 MT]).

Even though Israel's initial impulse is to go back to idolatry (2:7a [9a MT]), Yhwh will deliberately bring hardship (2:6, 9 [8, 11 MT]) to cause the people to finally seek him in desperation. Thus, this "returning" is described with the first occurrence of *shuv* in Hosea in 2:7 [9 MT]: "She shall pursue her lovers, but not overtake them; and she shall seek them, but shall not find them. Then she shall say, 'I will go and return [*shuv*] to my first husband, for it was better with me then than now.'" As one scholar explains, "Their refusal to repent would bring judgment from Yahweh, but this divine discipline and punishment is also what would cause Israel to 'return.'"[5] The opening section of Hosea (chs. 1–3) then closes with a dramatic prediction of struggle followed by renewal in 3:4–5: "For the Israelites shall remain many days without king or prince, without sacrifice or pillar, without ephod or teraphim. Afterward the Israelites shall return [*shuv*] and seek the Lord their God, and David their king; they shall come in awe to the Lord and to his goodness in the latter day." This promise of future faithfulness has been called "the pedagogical center for Hosea and the [Book of the Twelve]."[6] In other words, it is a key turning

---

4. The precise chronology and nature of the relationship between Hosea and Gomer, as well as the metaphorical import of the sexual imagery used throughout are highly disputed. For example, the adulterous wife and mother of Hos 2 could be correlated with the people of Israel, the land, Rachel, Asherah, or the city of Samaria (Kelle, *Hosea 2*, 81–90).

5. Yates, "Problem of Repentance and Relapse," 250.

6. Bowman, "Reading the Twelve as One," 56.

point for teaching Israel about their relationship with God. "[This] hinge . . . sets in motion what follows in Hosea and in the [Book of the Twelve]."[7] It is significant that this action of "return" involves "seeking" YHWH.[8]

Nonetheless, in the present experience of the prophet, sin has made the people's hearts unable to repent, as attested in 5:4: "Their deeds do not permit them to return [*shuv*] to their God. For the spirit of whoredom is within them, and they do not know the LORD." This creates tension with the calls for the people to repent and brings up "the question of the people's ability to hear and respond to the prophet's words."[9] Nonetheless, the prophet once again urges repentance in 6:1: "Come, let us return [*shuv*] to the LORD; for it is he who has torn, and he will heal us; he has struck down, and he will bind us up." Occurring closely afterwards is 6:3a "Let us know, let us press on to know the LORD." Just as we saw "seeking" being connected to returning in 3:5 above, here "returning" involves the action of "knowing." This points to "the covenantal relationship between the people and their God."[10] Unfortunately, the focus on condemnation of sin in the rest of the chapter (6:3–11) indicates that the nation is not receptive to this message, and for this reason, judgment is imminent.[11]

This exposition of disobedience continues in ch. 11. YHWH sadly reminisces that, although he led Israel out of Egypt, "they have refused to turn [*shuv*] to me" (11:5b) and "my people are bent on turning away from me" (11:7a). Nonetheless, YHWH has compassion on his people (11:8) and promises in 11:9a "I will not execute my fierce anger; I

7. Bowman, "Reading the Twelve as One," 56.
8. Boda, *Return to Me*, 96.
9. LeCureux, *Thematic Unity*, 236.
10. Boda, *Return to Me*, 96.
11. House, "Endings as New Beginnings," 319.

will not again [*shuv*] destroy Ephraim." This ability to show grace in the midst of rebellion "reveals an internal struggle within Yhwh (11.8–9) between his desire for holiness that would destroy unfaithful Israel, and his desire to forgive and to be once more restored to his people."[12]

The next significant call to repentance comes in 12:6 [7 MT]. After 12:1–5 [2–6 MT] recounts the need for Yhwh to punish Judah and retells Jacob's wrestling with the angel, v. 6 reads: "But as for you, return [*shuv*] to your God, hold fast to love and justice, and wait continually for your God." Here, the description of returning is fleshed out with maintaining "love" and "justice" as well as the action of "waiting."[13] But nonetheless the remainder of chs. 12 and 13 are filled with further descriptions of sin and punishment.

Hosea does end on a positive note with a final call to repentance in 14:1–2a [2–3a MT]: "Return [*shuv*], O Israel, to the Lord your God, for you have stumbled because of your iniquity. Take words with you and return [*shuv*] to the Lord." This is followed in vv. 4–7 [5–8 MT] with assurances of forgiveness and restoration of blessings. Crucially, in 14:3 [4 MT] the people confess that they will no longer look to Assyria or foreign gods for salvation but instead to Yhwh,[14] and as a result Yhwh promises in v. 4 [5 MT], "I will heal their disloyalty; I will love them freely, for my anger has turned [*shuv*] from them." One scholar insightfully summarizes this by stating "while the imperative calls to return are placed on the people, Yhwh himself also promises to respond to the people's return with a return of his own (14.5 [ET 14.4]), and thus is formed the

---

12. LeCureux, *Thematic Unity*, 236.
13. Boda, *Return to Me*, 96.
14. Boda, *Return to Me*, 96.

foundation for the Twelve's unifying concept of 'Return to me and I will return to you.'"[15]

JOEL

Three successive moments are crucial for understanding the theme of repentance and return in the book of Joel: the call to repentance in 2:12–14, the description of the rituals used to express that repentance in 2:15–17, and the divine response and description of restoration in 2:18—3:21 [4:21 MT].

Following the descriptions of devastation caused by a locust plague and enemy invasion in Joel 1:2—2:11, the prophet commands his audience to repent in 2:12–14:

> Yet even now, says the LORD, return [*shuv*] to me with all your heart, with fasting, with weeping, and with mourning; rend your hearts and not your clothing. Return [*shuv*] to the LORD, your God, for he is gracious and merciful, slow to anger, and abounding in steadfast love, and relents from punishing. Who knows whether he will not turn [*shuv*] and relent, and leave a blessing behind him, a grain offering and a drink offering for the LORD, your God?

Immediately there is a familiar echo of Hos 14:1–2a [2–3a MT] (see above), where *shuv* is also used twice to dramatically order the people to return to YHWH.[16] This call to repentance also evokes memories of the golden calf incident and its aftermath in Exod 32–34. After Moses intercedes for the people, he is commissioned to create two new tablets of the Ten Commandments (Exod 34:1–4) and YHWH comes to him, proclaiming his name and qualities (Exod 34:5–7). Joel 2:13b quotes from the list of attributes of YHWH given

15. LeCureux, *Thematic Unity*, 236.
16. Schart, "First Section," 142.

in Exod 34:6, "merciful and gracious, slow to anger, and abounding in steadfast love and faithfulness." A further connection between the two texts is that the word for "relent" in Joel 2:13, 14 is the same word used for Yhwh "changing his mind" in Exod 32:12, 14, when Moses convinces Yhwh to not annihilate the whole nation. This connection to Exodus in Joel is a reminder that reconciliation with Yhwh is still possible, and that "Yahweh would show mercy to the people of [Joel's] generation in the same way that he had in the early days of Israel's history at Mount Sinai."[17]

The expression of repentance in Joel 2:15–17 describes an assembly of the whole nation for a fast (vv. 15–16) while the priests, representing the people, pray the prayer found in 17b: "Spare your people, O Lord, and do not make your heritage a mockery, a byword among the nations. Why should it be said among the peoples, 'Where is their God?'" This prayer again points back to the golden calf episode (compare it with the prayer of Moses in Exod 32:11–14).[18] This ritual description gives specific content as to what it means to repent: "It at least begins with humility, fasting, prayer, and intercessory lament. It is not simply a psychological crisis that does not result in changed behavior."[19]

The subsequent section details what Yhwh's acceptance of this repentance looks like. In addition to agricultural blessings and bounty (2:19–26), Yhwh expresses his love to the people by giving them certain knowledge of Yhwh's presence and exclusivity (2:27). The rest of the book expands this restoration to include the Day of the Lord (covered in the next chapter) and the judgment of the other nations.

---

17. Yates, "Problem of Repentance and Relapse," 253.
18. Yates, "Problem of Repentance and Relapse," 253.
19. House, "Endings as New Beginnings," 322.

In this way, Joel shows us the contours of return and repentance in these three movements:

- God calls for repentance
- descriptions of the rituals of that repentance, and
- the people's experiences of God's provision and care upon their return.

AMOS

Where Hosea and Joel provided a mix of negative and positive pictures of return and repentance, Amos's vision is largely negative. Amos first mentions repentance with a negative example in ch. 4. Five times in a row Yhwh recounts a particular punishment he used to wake the people out of their spiritual stupor, always ending with the accusatory refrain "yet you did not return [*shuv*] to me" (4:6, 8, 9, 10, 11). Verse 9 mentions a locus plague as one of the punishments, introducing a deliberate contrast with Joel (see Joel 1). While the locust plague in Joel was successful in driving the people to repentance (see above), in Amos the people are so stubborn that even this does not motivate them to turn to Yhwh.[20] Read in progression with Hosea and Joel, it is notable that Amos no longer preaches that the people should repent, but instead "looks back on a history of failure to return,"[21] culminating in an ominous announcement, "prepare to meet your God, O Israel!" (4:12b).

Amos 5 becomes more hopeful about the possibility of reconciliation, with calls to "seek me and live" (v. 4) and "seek the Lord and live" (v. 6). In between these two commands is a contrasting negative imperative to *not* seek the

20. Yates, "Problem of Repentance and Relapse," 253.
21. Schart, "First Section," 144.

false worship taking place at the high places (v. 5). Idolatry will only result in exile (v. 5) and inherently involves social injustice: "Ah, you that turn justice to wormwood, and bring righteousness to the ground!" (v. 7). The same word for "seek" is used again in v. 14 in the phrase "Seek good and not evil, that you may live." This language is reminiscent of the connection between returning and seeking established earlier in Hos 3:5 (see above).[22] Another concrete action linked to repentance is identified in 5:15: "Hate evil and love good, and establish justice in the gate; it may be that the LORD, the God of hosts, will be gracious to the remnant of Joseph." With the potential of restoration hinted at by "it may be" in v. 15b, Amos reminds the reader of Joel 2:14a, "Who knows whether he will not turn and relent,"[23] although the subsequent exposition of the day of the LORD in Amos 5:18–20 is cast as being entirely negative for Israel (in contrast with the treatment of the same theme in Joel).

JONAH AND NAHUM

Jonah introduces a new aspect of repentance in the Book of the Twelve—the repentance of foreign nations. The previous books largely cast the nations in a negative light, but Jonah shows that the nations too can repent and be in right relationship with YHWH.[24] After Jonah's blatantly unhospitable announcement of imminent destruction in 3:4, the speech made by the king of Nineveh has notable parallels with the paradigm of repentance given in Joel 2:12–14. He calls for a fast in 3:7 (see Joel 2:12), and in 3:8b orders "All shall turn [*shuv*] from their evil ways and from the violence that is in their hands" (see Joel 2:12, 13). Next, in 3:9 the king asks

---

22. House, "Endings as New Beginnings," 325.
23. Yates, "Problem of Repentance and Relapse," 254–55.
24. House, "Endings as New Beginnings," 327.

"Who knows? God may relent [*shuv*] and change his mind; he may turn [*shuv*] from his fierce anger, so that we do not perish." (see Joel 2:14).[25] This proclamation also has similarities to Moses' prayer for the people in Exod 32:12 (a text mentioned in the discussion of Joel 2 above).[26] This hope of divine mercy is fulfilled in Jonah 3:10. When Yhwh sees "how they turned [*shuv*] from their evil ways, God changed his mind [also in v. 9] about the calamity that he had said he would bring upon them; and he did not do it." Upon seeing this display of God's grace, Jonah is furious even though he knows this is consistent with Yhwh's character. In Jonah 4:2 he quotes from Exod 34:6–7, but whereas Joel uses this quotation to speak hopefully, Jonah sees God's mercy and slowness to anger as failings. However, Yhwh's response in 4:11 makes it clear that "it was right for him to take pity on such an evil place when they turn from that evil."[27]

The example of Nineveh repenting serves as a reproach to Israel. Israel is without excuse. They have had multiple prophets reminding them to obey, but never exhibited such dramatic transformation as we see in Nineveh.[28] Of course, this transformation did not last long. Nahum, the very next book in the Twelve, focuses on Yhwh's judgment on Assyria.[29] Even though the book of Jonah shows that repentance is always possible, Nahum, conversely, means that punishment for sin is always possible too: "repentance is not a one-time event that precludes judgment for centuries. Sin must cease or be repented of for mercy to continue."[30]

---

25. Yates, "Problem of Repentance and Relapse," 258.
26. Boda, *Return to Me*, 99.
27. House, "Endings as New Beginnings," 327.
28. Yates, "Problem of Repentance and Relapse," 259.
29. Yates, "Problem of Repentance and Relapse," 259.
30. House, "Endings as New Beginnings," 328.

MICAH AND ZEPHANIAH

Micah touches on repentance in 6:6–8, as the prophet takes on the voice of a person wishing to be right with God. He asks how to "come" or "bow" before God (v. 6) and if his "transgression" or "sin of [his] soul" (v. 7) must be atoned for with conventional offerings from the sacrificial system (vv. 6b–7). The answer comes in the well-known v. 8, to "do justice, and to love kindness, and to walk humbly with your God." As we have seen above, true contrition involves the loving actions and heart attitudes established in Yhwh's covenant.[31] As noted in the discussion of Amos above, the earlier outright calls for repentance found in Hosea and Joel are even more muted here, as Micah simply models confession of sin and acceptance of deserved judgment in 7:9: "I must bear the indignation of the Lord, because I have sinned against him, until he takes my side and executes judgment for me. He will bring me out to the light; I shall see his vindication." In Mic 7:10, the people's enemies ask, "Where is the Lord your God?" While a similar question was present in Joel 2:17, Micah merely hopes for a future time when Israel's enemies no longer ask that question, rather than recording immediate deliverance.[32]

The final lines of Micah quote from Exod 34:6–7 (as found in Joel and Jonah), but in this case there is no immediate act of repentance by the people or expectation of release from punishment: "Who is a God like you, pardoning iniquity and passing over the transgression of the remnant of your possession? He does not retain his anger forever, because he delights in showing clemency. He will again have compassion upon us; he will tread our iniquities under foot" (Mic 7:18–19a). Nonetheless, this recitation

---

31. Boda, *Return to Me*, 100.
32. Yates, "Problem of Repentance and Relapse," 256.

of Yhwh's nature "reflects the hope that Yahweh's mercy would ultimately triumph over his judgment."[33]

This greatly diminished expectation of immediate deliverance only decreases further as we need to move past Nahum and Habakkuk into Zephaniah to find anything relevant to repentance. Zephaniah 2:3 reads "Seek the Lord, all you humble of the land, who do his commands; seek righteousness, seek humility; perhaps you may be hidden on the day of the Lord's wrath." Here, the pious remnant is advised to "seek" Yhwh (a term often associated with repentance as seen above) so that they may merely be preserved through the terrifying judgment of the day of Yhwh. The punishment of the nation as a whole is inevitable.[34]

HAGGAI

Haggai starts with a problem: the exile is over and the people are once again living in the land of Judah, but the people have neglected to rebuild the temple of Yhwh. As a result, God has afflicted their agricultural efforts (1:2–11). In this setting, the people demonstrate repentance by "obeying" and "fearing" Yhwh (1:12). As a result, Haggai assures the people that Yhwh is present with them (1:13), and Yhwh "stirs up" the spirits of the leaders and the people, enabling them to work on the temple (1:14). This demonstration of obedience in building the temple leads to a promise of blessing and prosperity from Yhwh (2:7–9). It is notable that both the mode of prodding the people to repentance and the precise type of obedience required differ from what we have seen previously. There are no threats of the day of

---

33. Yates, "Problem of Repentance and Relapse," 256.
34. House, "Endings as New Beginnings," 332–33.

Yhwh, and, rather than responding with cultic observances and social justice, the people are required to build.[35]

ZECHARIAH

Zechariah opens with a call to repentance and a positive response. In Zech 1:3, the prophet relates the divine word to the people, "Return [*shuv*] to me, says the Lord of hosts, and I will return [*shuv*] to you, says the Lord of hosts" (compare with the similar phrases in Hosea and Joel). The prophet warns his audience not to follow the examples of earlier generations who ignored the call to return (vv. 4–6a). Happily, 1:6b reports "So they repented [*shuv*]" and the people acknowledge Yhwh's justice in the punishment he had previously administered.[36] As a result, the subsequent vision of Zechariah reports that Yhwh has likewise "returned" to the people in 1:16a: "Therefore, thus says the Lord, I have returned to Jerusalem with compassion; my house shall be built in it." However, as we progress through the next several chapters (see especially ch. 7), it is clear that the people are not fully obedient. Zechariah 8:16–17 gives a renewed description of what repentance should look like: "These are the things that you shall do: Speak the truth to one another, render in your gates judgments that are true and make for peace, do not devise evil in your hearts against one another, and love no false oath; for all these are things that I hate, says the Lord." As a result of this change, the promised blessings in 8:18–23 include a future filled with feasting instead of fasting, and the nations being drawn to worship Yhwh.

However, more judgments for disobedience await the reader who continues through Zechariah. As a result,

35. House, "Endings as New Beginnings," 334.
36. Boda, *Return to Me*, 102.

in 12:10 Yhwh promises to do something entirely new to remedy the problem of sin: "And I will pour out a spirit of compassion and supplication on the house of David and the inhabitants of Jerusalem, so that, when they look on the one whom they have pierced, they shall mourn for him, as one mourns for an only child, and weep bitterly over him, as one weeps over a firstborn." This "pouring out" of the spirit as part of the time of "restoration" reminds us of Joel 2:28–29.[37] This will cause all the people to mourn deeply (vv. 11–14). Yhwh's next step to ensuring lasting repentance is in 13:1: "On that day a fountain shall be opened for the house of David and the inhabitants of Jerusalem, to cleanse them from sin and impurity." If all this was not enough, Yhwh will also permanently eradicate idols and false prophets (13:2–6). This all-encompassing transformation goes far beyond the guidelines and promises given in the previous books of the Twelve, as "the people are changed, Jerusalem is holy, and the Lord has returned to the people who have returned to him."[38] Nonetheless, as we think in terms of the Twelve, we must still consider the witness of Malachi in relation to Zechariah.

MALACHI

Malachi contains a call to return that closely echoes the words of Zech 1:3 (and, of course, the earlier relevant texts from Hosea and Joel). Malachi 3:7 reads "Ever since the days of your ancestors you have turned aside from my statutes and have not kept them. Return [*shuv*] to me, and I will return [*shuv*] to you, says the Lord of hosts. But you say, 'How shall we return [*shuv*]?'" Although Malachi's community was characterized by those who withheld tithes and

37. Boda, *Return to Me*, 104.
38. House, "Endings as New Beginnings," 336.

saw little benefit in obedience (3:8–15), Yʜᴡʜ commends those who "revere" and "think on" his name (3:16). This is reminiscent of Zephaniah, where it is only a remnant that respond, rather than all the people.[39]

Malachi ends with an announcement of the Day of Yʜᴡʜ, when "all the arrogant and all evildoers will be stubble; the day that comes shall burn them up, says the Lᴏʀᴅ of hosts, so that it will leave them neither root nor branch" (4:1 [3:19 MT]). Then, after a command to obey the teaching of Moses (4:4 [3:22 MT]) and a notice that the prophet Elijah will come before the day of Yʜᴡʜ (4:5 [3:23 MT]), Malachi explains what this future Elijah will do: "He will turn [*shuv*] the hearts of parents to their children and the hearts of children to their parents, so that I will not come and strike the land with a curse" (4:6 [3:24 MT]). Through the ministry of this prophet, the people will be enabled to "turn" their hearts in the necessary way to avoid the destruction described in 4:1 [3:19 MT]. The day of Yʜᴡʜ (discussed in the next chapter) makes possible the kind of fresh start that rituals and efforts to do good could not accomplish. Much like the pouring out of the spirit and opening of the fountain of cleansing in Zech 12–13, here, "regardless of the people's choice, the Lᴏʀᴅ will remove sin and restore the humble of the land to their rightful place in Zion."[40]

VIEWING THE BIG PICTURE

As we have seen, the big picture of repentance in the Book of the Twelve has taken a U-shaped path, from the early summons to return to Yʜᴡʜ in Hosea and Joel, to the absence of such calls and the abandonment of the hope of avoiding punishment in Amos, Micah, and

39. Yates, "Problem of Repentance and Relapse," 260.
40. House, "Endings as New Beginnings," 337.

Repentance and Return

Zephaniah, to the renewed call for repentance and hope of Yhwh intervening to make true transformation possible in Zechariah and Malachi. However, the picture at the end of Malachi is ambivalent enough to allow other interpretations. One other frame for this topic would be to organize the text into three movements of "repentance" followed by "relapse." First, Joel describes true repentance, with Amos, Micah, Habakkuk, and Zephaniah gradually extinguishing the possibility of the people turning in time to avoid exile. Second, the people of Nineveh function as a counter-example of repentance in Jonah, but in Nahum they too relapse and suffer punishment. Third, Haggai and Zechariah give positive examples of restoration, but Malachi only describes an incomplete return to obedience and ends with a reminder of the coming judgment.[41]

Another important clue to the structure of this theme across the Twelve comes from viewing the distribution of the word *shuv* ("turn, return"). All of the imperative forms of this verb, a verbal form associated with a request or command, occur in the first two (Hosea, Joel) and last two (Zechariah, Malachi) books of the Twelve in the similar calls to "return" to Yhwh that have been noted above.[42] Placing these phrases in succession allows one to see their linear development. Hosea 14:1–2 [2–3 MT] states "Return, O Israel, to the Lord your God . . . return to the Lord," while Joel 2:12–13 becomes more personal by placing the divine voice in the first person: "return to me with all your heart. . . . Return to the Lord, your God." Joel serves as a bridge between the commands in Hosea and the reciprocal phrases that also contain divine "turning" in both Zechariah and Malachi.[43] These are found in Zech 1:3, "Return to

---

41. Yates, "Problem of Repentance and Relapse," 251.
42. LeCureux, *Thematic Unity*, 22.
43. LeCureux, *Thematic Unity*, 236.

me... and I will return to you," and Mal 3:7, "Return to me, and I will return to you."

Furthermore, out of the eighty-four times different forms of this verb appear in the Twelve, twenty-two occur in Hosea[44] and fifteen in Amos (as part of the first three books of the Twelve), along with seventeen in Zechariah and seven in Malachi (the last two books of the Twelve). This gives further evidence of a U-shaped focus on repentance that opens and closes the Twelve.

CONCLUSION

This chapter has examined the diverse contours of what it means for the people and Yhwh to "return" to each other in the Twelve. As we have seen, elements associated with repentance include turning from different kinds of sin, performing various rituals, and being transformed internally.[45] Yhwh, for his part, is not entirely predictable, and the people must always be somewhat uncertain about whether or not punishment can be avoided: "Yhwh always remains dangerous; he is capable of ignoring his people's pleas for repentance and bringing about untold destruction,"[46] but at the same time, it is Yhwh who will take the initiative to make possible the cleansing of the people's hearts so they can enjoy the blessings of restoration.[47] The Twelve leaves us with the hope that if the people return to God and repent, God will ultimately return to them.

---

44. This may be 24 depending on how one analyzes the text.
45. Boda, *Return to Me*, 106.
46. LeCureux, *Thematic Unity*, 240.
47. House, "Endings as New Beginnings," 337–38.

REFLECTION QUESTIONS:

1. Based on your readings, what does it mean to "return" to the LORD? How is this related to "repentance"?
2. How is Joel different from some of the other books in the Twelve on this topic?
3. If you were going to draw the developing picture of the idea of repentance and return in the Twelve, what would it look like?
4. How does what you have read about repentance in this chapter compare to what you have heard about repentance in the past, whether in your Christian context or in Scripture itself?

5

THE DAY OF THE LORD

INTRODUCTION

THE DAY OF THE LORD is one of the most prevalent yet controversial themes in the Book of the Twelve. Part of the reason for this is how the New Testament uses elements from the Twelve in its announcements of the Day of the LORD. Many Christians find the Day of the LORD mysterious and confusing today. In this chapter, we will first discuss criteria for detecting references to the Day of the LORD. Next, we will briefly cover some of the questions the New Testament raises about the Day of the LORD. Finally, we will explore how the Day of the LORD shows up throughout the Twelve and concisely summarize the meaning and purpose of this concept.

The Day of the Lord

WHAT CONSTITUTES A REFERENCE TO THE DAY OF THE LORD?

One of the complications around the Day of the Lord comes from the struggle to agree on what counts as a reference to the "Day of the Lord." Scholars differ on what counts as the right criteria for judging such a reference. As we will see below, there are many places the prophets use the phrase "on that day" rather than the full expression "the Day of the Lord." Should the former count as authentic references?

Scholars sit across a wide spectrum in their ways of answering the question above. On one end of the spectrum, some scholars believe that the phrase "Day of the Lord" is not a "term" at all, in the sense of having a technical or fixed meaning, but that it simply points to any day that Yhwh influences in some way.[1] As a result, the abstract concept that we call the "Day of the Lord" could be connected to any account of Yhwh appearing and acting, regardless of the precise language used.[2] On the opposite end of the spectrum, other scholars believe that "Day of the Lord" and its related phrases should be understood as pointing to a specific concept. As this concept developed over time, it acquired an eschatological meaning, pointing to an end-time expectation.[3]

For our chapter, we take a middle of the spectrum approach. For us, to say a reference is about "the Day of the Lord," it needs to have both of the following two factors: (1) It needs to use the actual word "day," and (2) The word "day" needs to be used in a context that is plausibly referencing the future. This allows us to avoid being overwhelmed by

1. Ishai-Rosenboim, "Term," 400.
2. Ishai-Rosenboim, "Term," 401.
3. Hoffman, "Day of the Lord," 49.

every possible text that relates to an appearance of Yhwh, yet still not be so rigid as to exclude everything except the precise phrase "Day of the Lord."

THE DAY OF THE LORD AND THE NEW TESTAMENT

While this chapter is focused on the Day of the Lord in the Book of the Twelve, as Christians we cannot easily escape the tendency to read these Old Testament descriptions of the Day of the Lord with a New Testament lens. This means that many Christians automatically import categories they are familiar with from the New Testament (or even systematic theology) even as they are studying the Old Testament uses of this phrase. For some, this leads immediately to discussions of the "end times." For instance, for scholars following the paradigm of dispensational premillennialism (a particular theological belief about the "end times"),[4] this can lead to Old Testament

---

4. Dispensationalism is a system for understanding the relationship between the Old and New Testaments. It emphasizes the different ways in which God related to his people over time. For example, the expectations for obedience changed when the Mosaic law was given. A crucial distinction made in dispensationalism is between Israel and the church. The promises of the Old Testament regarding national Israel will be consummated in national Israel in the future, rather than being fulfilled in the church. See Erickson, *Christian Theology*, 1168–69. Amongst the range of Christian views on eschatology (i.e., things to come in the future) dispensationalists are premillennialists, that is, they believe that Jesus will come back to earth, then reign for a thousand years prior to The End (Grenz, *Theology*, 615). As compared to other premillennialists, dispensationalists specifically hold that the church will be raptured, or suddenly taken up to heaven, prior to the tribulation, an intensive, seven-year period of judgment. At the end of the tribulation, Jesus will overthrow the forces of evil and national Israel will be blessed, fulfilling all the Old Testament prophecies of renewal, during his thousand-year reign on

references to the Day of the LORD being shoehorned into the structure of rapture-tribulation-millennium central to their theological framework, with two different Days of the LORD happening at the end of the tribulation and just before the creation of the new earth.[5]

For this reason, it is helpful for us to take a moment to see how the New Testament uses this phrase. Careful consideration of the relevant New Testament texts shows that the usage of this concept is far more fluid than the dispensational scholarship above suggests. In many places in the New Testament, the "Day of the LORD" is an event that will come in the future (Phil 1:6). It includes judgement of the righteous and the wicked (Rom 2:5, 16; 1 Cor 1:8; 5:5; 2 Cor 1:14; 2 Tim 4:8; 2 Pet 2:9) and destruction of the physical creation (2 Pet 3:10). It will come suddenly in a time of apparent peace (1 Thess 5:2–3), but is also preceded by rebellion (2 Thess 2:2–3). However, in Acts 2:14–24, we see a more present sense of the Day of the LORD. Here in his sermon on the Day of Pentecost, Peter quotes Joel 2:28–32 [3:1–5 MT]. Peter's sermon connects the fulfilment of Joel's prophecy with the inauguration of the church after the ascension of Christ. He seems to be declaring that the Day of the LORD is happening on that very day, in front of the people on Pentecost. This shows that the Day of the LORD is "inextricably linked with the word of Jesus Christ and the inauguration of his kingdom,"[6] but cannot be narrowly read as a reference to what is commonly understood as "the end times." Instead, the earthly ministry of Jesus Christ begins a kind of "end times" that inaugurates his kingdom, which will be fulfilled in his second coming.

---

earth. See Grenz, *Theology*, 616–17.

5. Mayhue, "Prophet's Watchword," 246.

6. Barker, "Day of the Lord," 142.

As we can see from this brief survey, the New Testament does not provide us with only one way of understanding the Day of the Lord. As it is written after the coming of Jesus, it is shaped by the experience of Jesus's death and resurrection and the implications for God's people. While these questions of New Testament theology (and eschatology) are important, we will show in this chapter that to understand the Day of the Lord in the Twelve it helps to keep the immediate audience of the ancient prophets in mind. By first sharpening our understanding of the portraits of the Day of the Lord in the conceptual environment of the Old Testament and specifically the Twelve, we will be better equipped to grapple with the New Testament's understanding and deployment of these passages.

THE DAY OF THE LORD IN THE BOOK OF THE TWELVE

This examination of the Day of the Lord in the Twelve assumes the criteria we discussed earlier. We have thus limited our discussion below to the books within the Twelve that include the term "day" with a future aspect and are clearly associated with the actions of the Lord in some way. It is important to note that the Day of the Lord appears elsewhere in Old Testament as well. Its occurrences in the Major Prophets (such as in Isa 34:8 and Ezek 7:19) are also important for understanding what the Old Testament says about the Day of the Lord as a whole.[7]

---

7. See Barker, "Day of the Lord," 137–38.

Joel

Joel has a higher density of references to the Day of the LORD than any other Old Testament text.[8] Joel 1 begins by describing a devastating plague of locusts in vv. 2–12, followed by a summons to repentance in vv. 13–14. However, v. 15 indicates that something even worse lies ahead: "Alas for the day! For the day of the LORD is near, and as destruction from the Almighty it comes."[9] In the midst of extensive agricultural devastation, Joel begs YHWH for relief (1:19–20), as YHWH is the only one who can provide shelter on his day.[10] Joel 2:1–11 moves on from the focus on rural areas in ch. 1, and lists consequences of the Day of the LORD for Jerusalem.[11] 2:11b states "Truly the day of the LORD is great; terrible indeed—who can endure it?" This turn to the direct threat of "divine judgment" makes even the possibility of enemy invasion seem less important.[12] This is followed by a call to repentance (2:12–17) and a promise from YHWH to restore the land and be present with his people (2:18–27).

In 2:28 [3:1 MT], which simply begins "Then afterward," the subsequent section looks to the future and the nature of the Day becomes more positive for Judah.[13] Although there will be cosmic disturbances "before the great and terrible day of the LORD comes" (2:31 [3:4 MT]), details immediately emerge of salvation coming for those who turned to YHWH ("Then everyone who calls on the name of the LORD shall be saved," 2:32 [3:5 MT]), along

8. Jeremias, "Function of the Book of Joel," 78.
9. Bakon, "Day of the Lord," 150.
10. House, "Endings as New Beginnings," 321.
11. House, "Endings as New Beginnings," 321–22.
12. Andiñach, "Latin American Approaches," 430.
13. House, "Endings as New Beginnings," 323.

with an outpouring of Yhwh's spirit (2:28 [3:1 MT]), and punishment for the nations (3:12 [4:12 MT]).[14] This gifting of the spirit to all genders, ages, and social classes (2:28–29 [3:1–2 MT]) is notable, as it points towards "the possibility of a different society . . . [not] only to liberation from foreign powers . . . [but also] the internal situation, too. The undervalued sectors of society are the ones that will transmit the word of God."[15]

The motifs of cosmic disturbance in 3:15–16a [4:15–16a MT] echo the earlier descriptions of judgment against Jerusalem in 2:10–11.[16] One scholar has observed that Joel exhibits a progression "from presumed judgment to a call for repentance, to promised restoration, to judgment on the nations who oppressed Judah and Jerusalem."[17] Put differently, "oppression is not God's final word for the people."[18]

The end result of this future Day of the Lord will be universal knowledge of Yhwh's sole lordship (3:17 [4:17 MT]), the consecration and restoration of the fertility of the land "in that day" (3:17–18 [4:17–18 MT], a reversal of the devastation of Joel 1),[19] and the dwelling of the people in Judah (3:20 [4:20 MT]).[20]

With the big picture of the theme of the Day of the Lord in Joel in view, one very important point emerges: "the book of Joel (ch. 1–2) is *the only book in the Old Testament daring to speak of the survival of a whole generation in Israel in the context of the Day of the Lord.*"[21] As we

14. Bakon, "Day of the Lord," 150.
15. Andiñach, "Latin American Approaches," 434.
16. Werse, "Joel, Catchwords, and Its Place," 552.
17. Nogalski, "Day(s) of Yhwh," 200.
18. Andiñach, "Latin American Approaches," 428.
19. Werse, "Joel, Catchwords, and Its Place," 552.
20. House, "Endings as New Beginnings," 323.
21. Jeremias, "Function of the Book of Joel," 78. Italics original.

move forward through the rest of the Twelve, in the midst of far more pessimistic portraits of the Day of the LORD, the presentation of Joel always reminds us that there ultimately will be a positive outcome for those who have come to repentance, and it thus functions as a "hermeneutical key to the Twelve."[22]

Amos

Whereas Joel ends on a hopeful note regarding the Day of the LORD, Amos's picture seems on the surface far less positive and likely historically earlier than Joel's picture. Amos's classic warning of the coming Day of the LORD occurs in 5:18–20. Even though Joel is placed before Amos in the Hebrew canonical order, in historical terms this part of Amos almost certainly precedes Joel. Because of this Amos is generally considered to have the earliest reference to the Day of the LORD in the Old Testament.[23] Amos 5:18–20 states, "Alas for you who desire the day of the LORD! Why do you want the day of the LORD? It is darkness, not light; as if someone fled from a lion, and was met by a bear; or went into the house and rested a hand against the wall, and was bitten by a snake. Is not the day of the LORD darkness, not light, and gloom with no brightness in it?" This threat was delivered to the northern kingdom during a time when the people were greatly disobedient (5:12) but nonetheless assumed that YHWH supported them (5:14). Amos 5:18–20 informs them that, contrary to their expectations, the Day of the LORD would signify disaster for *them*, not their enemies.[24] The descriptions of "darkness" (vv. 18, 20) and "gloom" (v. 20) are similar

22. Jeremias, "Function of the Book of Joel," 77.
23. Nogalski, "Day(s) of Yhwh," 204.
24. Mayhue, "Prophet's Watchword," 238.

to those found in Joel 2:2.²⁵ As noted in chapter 4 above, though, Joel prods the southern kingdom to repent prior to the Day of the Lord, but in contrast, "The day of Yhwh in Amos 5:18–20 is again directed toward the northern kingdom, but it presumes the day of judgment will result from Israel's refusal to return to Yhwh."²⁶

The theme of the Day of the Lord returns in Amos 8. After recounting more of the people's sins (8:4–6), the word "day" (*yom*) occurs five times from vv. 9–13, as Yhwh promises darkness (v. 9, reminiscent of 5:18, 20) and mourning (v. 10), ending with the "deepest consequence"²⁷ of the absence of the prophetic word (vv. 11–12) and the consequent spiritual starvation of the people (vv. 13–14).

In Amos 9:11, the phrase "on that day" introduces a promise of restoration (vv. 11–15) that concludes the book. It is worth noting the language of bountiful wine in 9:13b, which echoes imagery already used in Joel 3:18a [4:18a MT]. Although the people are depicted as unrepentant and judgment is inevitable (9:8–10), there nonetheless will be a future time of renewal after the dreadful punishment of the Day itself.²⁸ As one scholar states, "If the prophets' efforts fail due to lack of returning, the day of the Lord itself will effect a new beginning. The day purges sin from the people and leaves persons like the prophets as representatives of the living God."²⁹

---

25. Nogalski, "Day(s) of Yhwh," 204.
26. Nogalski, "Day(s) of Yhwh," 205.
27. Bulkeley, "Book of Amos," 168.
28. Bulkeley, "Book of Amos," 169.
29. House, "Endings as New Beginnings," 325.

Obadiah

The first part of the short book of Obadiah predicts destruction for Edom (vv. 1–9) because of its failure to assist Judah (vv. 10–14) when it was invaded (presumably in the Babylonian exile of 587).[30] Although the full phrase "Day of the Lord" first appears in v. 15, attentive readers will notice that the word "day" (*yom*) itself occurs before v. 15. In fact, it occurs ten times in vv. 11–14 to describe Judah's devastation as happening on a particular "day." Readers attentive to this language and the larger canonical witness will naturally associate this use of "day" with other descriptions of judgments of Judah on the Day of the Lord. While many English translations render this as something that has happened in the past, (for example, 14a: "You should not have stood at the crossings to cut off his fugitives" [NRSV, so also CEB, KJV, NET, NIV, JPS]), the Hebrew forms used could also be rendered as commands about a future event (again, 14a: "Do not stand at the crossroads to eliminate their survivors" [NASB, so also ESV and HCSB]). As one scholar explains "These verses convey this message using linguistic forms that display a bifurcated sense of time. . . . Obad[iah] 12–14 uses the syntax of negative commands + imperfect, whose chronological perspective assumes they are issued prior to an event. However, Obad 11 and 15 demonstrate knowledge that Edom *has already* done what vv. 12–14 say not to do."[31] Since Obadiah comes after Amos, it is interesting that the warnings to Edom in Obadiah are similar to the warnings to Israel in Amos.[32]

Obadiah 15–16 point to the Day of the Lord being a reality that will face all the nations who opposed God's

---

30. House, "Endings as New Beginnings," 326.
31. Nogalski, "Day(s) of Yhwh," 208.
32. Nogalski, "Day(s) of Yhwh," 209.

people: "For the day of the LORD is near against all the nations. As you have done, it shall be done to you; your deeds shall return on your own head. For as you have drunk on my holy mountain, all the nations around you shall drink; they shall drink and gulp down, and shall be as though they had never been." Notice that the idea that the Day of the LORD is "near" echoes a refrain from Joel (Joel 1:15; 2:1; 3:14 [4:14 MT]).[33] The remainder of Obadiah (vv. 17–21) prophesies salvation for Israel and its possession of the land. It is particularly notable that v. 18 mentions both the "house of Jacob" and the "house of Joseph," as this imagines a time that the two kingdoms will be re-united after the Day of the LORD.[34]

Obadiah's three-part structure of linear judgment against Edom, Judah, and the nations[35] leads one scholar to see the uses of "day" against both Edom (vv. 8–9) and Judah (vv. 10–14) as creating a literary tension that builds into the temporal ambiguity inherent in vv. 12–14. This tension is resolved in vv. 15–18, which involves both parties and time references:

> The description of "the day" spoke of the past transgressions Edom inflicted upon his brother Jacob. While at the same time, *lex talionis*[36] reveals that those descriptions are likewise articulations of what is to come in Edom's future "day." There is one "day of the LORD." This one symbol is experienced by Jacob in the past at the hand of

33. Nogalski, "Day(s) of Yhwh," 211.

34. Nogalski, "Day(s) of Yhwh," 211.

35. Nogalski, "Day(s) of Yhwh," 212.

36. *Lex Talionis* refers to the laws of retribution found in Exod 21:24–25, Lev 24:20, and Deut 19:21, in which someone who injured another person would themselves be injured the same way in punishment. This is often summarized in the popular expression "an eye for an eye, a tooth for a tooth."

Edom, and will be experienced by Edom in the future as divine judgment.[37]

In other words, Yhwh's work in the "Day of the Lord" results in multiple manifestations. In Obadiah, these include suffering that Jacob experienced at the hands of Edom, as well as the similar devastation that Edom later experienced. In this way, Obadiah gives us a picture of the Day of the Lord impacted by the past and pointed towards the future.

Zephaniah

From Obadiah's tri-partite judgment of the Day of the Lord on Edom, Judah, and the nations, we move to Zephaniah's version of the Day of the Lord, which gives a universal picture of God's judgment on that day. Zephaniah begins with a shocking announcement: "I will utterly sweep away everything from the face of the earth, says the Lord" (1:2; cf. 1:18). This universal judgment quickly turns into a specific rebuke of Judah, citing its sins of idolatry (1:4–6) and oppression (1:9). Zephaniah 1:7 and 1:14 clarify that this catastrophe is itself the Day of the Lord. Where 1:7 explains that "the day of the Lord is at hand," 1:14 builds on this stating that "The great day of the Lord is near, near and hastening fast; the sound of the day of the Lord is bitter, the warrior cries aloud there." Verse 15 fleshes out this picture with a string of stunningly negative descriptors: "That day will be a day of wrath, a day of distress and anguish, a day of ruin and devastation, a day of darkness and gloom, a day of clouds and thick darkness." The word "day" is used over and over with terms that bring clarity to its content. Zephaniah promises "a full, a terrible end [Yhwh] will make of all the inhabitants of the earth" (1:18). This incorporation

---

37. Werse, "Obadiah's 'Day of the Lord,'" 123.

of "finality and extinction" provides an "eschatological nuance"[38] and is reminiscent of Isa 2:12–22.

In Zeph 2:1–3, the focus shifts to practical steps the people can take. They should "gather" (Zeph 2:1) and "seek" Yhwh, as well as "righteousness" and "humility" (2:3), but it is meanwhile a foregone conclusion that "there comes upon you the day of the Lord's wrath" (2:2). The best that the people can hope for is that "perhaps you may be hidden on the day of the Lord's wrath" (2:3). The ones who are "humble" in Judah "will be preserved, but the nation will not. . . . The time has passed for a more general seeking and finding of the Lord."[39]

At this point, Zephaniah transitions to words of judgment against different nations (2:4–15), before again recounting the sins of Jerusalem (3:1–7) and promising global punishment (3:8, using "day"). Significantly, "Never to this point has the Book of the Twelve offered such a picture of worldwide judgment."[40] After all this, there will be a time of cleansing renewal (3:9–13; v. 11 uses "on that day") and rejoicing for Judah (3:14–20; v. 16 again uses "on that day"). This restoration ends Zephaniah on a positive note. As one scholar notes, "Zephaniah acts as a summary of how judgment comes to Israel and the nations without that judgment being the final word. Renewal is the final word, and that word may well have encouraged the Twelve's first audience."[41] Zephaniah is able to depict dramatic judgment coming upon Israel and the nations, but it still ends with a vision of restoration. Thus, while Zephaniah's picture of the Day of the Lord involves a universal

---

38. Hoffman, "Day of the Lord," 46.
39. House, "Endings as New Beginnings," 333.
40. House, "Endings as New Beginnings," 333.
41. House, "Endings as New Beginnings," 333.

picture of judgment, his final word about the Day of the LORD is one of encouragement.

Zechariah

Whereas other books we have examined thus far in the Twelve have tended to use the Day of the Twelve as a *judgment* day for Israel/Judah and the nations, the first thirteen chapters of Zechariah use the phrase "on that day" a number of times to indicate future acts of *restoration* (2:15; 3:10; 9:16; 12:3, 4, 6, 8, 9, 11; 13:1, 2, 4; cf. "those days" in 8:23). These scenarios include other nations worshipping YHWH (2:15), agricultural prosperity for Judah (3:10), judgment for nations that oppressed Judah (12:9), and the removal of idolatry from Judah (13:2). As compared to what we read in the previous books in the Twelve, the Day of the LORD now functions specifically to protect Judah, rather than merely being a means of eliminating its enemies.[42] Because some scholars have felt the need for the Day of the LORD to only mean one thing in every context in which it is invoked, these scholars have erroneously argued that the Day of the LORD is only an act of judgment, with any blessing for Judah coming *after* the Day and strictly not being part of it.[43] However, Zech 14:1 specifically mentions the Day of the LORD ("a day is coming for the LORD," NRSV), and the word "day" subsequently occurs eleven more times throughout ch. 14.

Zechariah 14's exposition of the *effects* of the Day of the LORD can be divided into five parts.[44] First, the nations will raze Jerusalem and deport half of the inhabitants (14:1–2). Second, YHWH comes to his peoples' aid, using

42. House, "Endings as New Beginnings," 335.
43. As seen in Mayhue, "Prophet's Watchword," 242.
44. Boda, *Haggai, Zechariah*, 71.

an earthquake to split the Mount of Olives, so as to provide a path for the peoples' escape and for his entrance into the battle (14:3–5).[45] Third, the created order is transformed so that there is endless daylight (14:7, cf. Isa 60:19)[46] and abundant waters will flow from Jerusalem (14:8). This is the result of Yhwh taking kingship over the entire earth. His name is described as "one" (14:9; cf. Deut 6:4), indicating he is the sole recipient of all worship.[47] Additionally, Jerusalem will be elevated over the surrounding area (14:10) and will never again experience the exterminating *herem*[48] judgment that was part of the conquest of Canaan (14:11).[49] Fourth, Yhwh will decisively defeat the nations who attacked Jerusalem (14:12–15): "On that day a great panic from the Lord shall fall on them" (v. 13a). As part of this, Jerusalem will inherit the wealth of the nations (v. 14). Fifth and finally, all the survivors from the nations will regularly visit Jerusalem to celebrate the feast of booths (also known as Tabernacles), and they will experience plagues if they do not participate (14:16–19). The temple in Jerusalem will be fully consecrated, with all of its utensils being fully holy: "On that day there shall be inscribed on the bells of the horses, 'Holy to the Lord.' And the cooking pots in the house of the Lord shall be as holy as the bowls in front of the altar" (14:20). This status was previously only written "on the head plate of the high priest

---

45. Boda, *Haggai, Zechariah*, 524.

46. Boda, *Haggai, Zechariah*, 525.

47. Boda, *Haggai, Zechariah*, 526.

48. The *herem* (or "ban") essentially refers to things that were devoted to Yhwh by complete destruction. In the context of warfare, this destruction served the purpose of judgment. Instructions for *herem* warfare in the conquest of Canaan occur in Deut 20:16–18. See Creach, *Joshua*, 8.

49. Boda, *Haggai, Zechariah*, 527.

(Ex. 28:36–38)."[50] The book of Zechariah ends with "And there shall no longer be traders in the house of the Lord of hosts on that day" (14:21b). This teaches that there would be no more need for businesspeople to sell implements or offerings in the temple course (Mark 11:15), an endeavor that often exploited the customers.[51]

This description of a renewed state where Judah's relationships with both Yhwh and the nations are ideal leaves the reader with a sense of finality. However, the Book of the Twelve is not yet over, as Malachi also comments on the Day of the Lord.[52]

Malachi

Whereas Zechariah focuses extensively on restoration in his Day of the Lord passages, Malachi emphasizes precisely how contingent these promises of the Day of the Lord are on the people's response to God's calls to them via the prophets. Malachi 3:1 promises that Yhwh will come to his temple, and that a "messenger of the covenant" will "prepare the way." The next verse (3:2) points to the Day of the Lord, stating "But who can endure the day of his coming, and who can stand when he appears? For he is like a refiner's fire and like fullers' soap." The results of this visitation are first experienced by the priests (3:3–4) who will be purified and enabled to properly carry out their offerings: "The purification will enable the priesthood as a whole to function anew and the future sacrifices of Judah will be pleasing to Yahweh, as they were of old."[53] Next, in 3:5 Yhwh promises to execute judgment against the people

50. Boda, *Haggai, Zechariah*, 528.
51. Boda, *Haggai, Zechariah*, 529.
52. House, "Endings as New Beginnings," 336.
53. Boloje and Groenewald, "Day of Yahweh," 70.

who practice various sins. In stating "I will be swift to bear witness," Yhwh indicates that he is "both a witness and a judge" in this scenario.[54]

In 3:17, Malachi's tone becomes more hopeful with "They shall be mine, says the LORD of hosts, my special possession on the day when I act, and I will spare them as parents spare their children who serve them." The final section of the book further develops contrasting outcomes for the righteous and wicked on the Day of the LORD. It begins with 4:1a [3:19a MT] "See, the day is coming, burning like an oven, when all the arrogant and all evildoers will be stubble." Conversely, those "who revere my name" will "go out leaping like calves from the stall" (4:2 [3:20 MT]). Furthermore, the righteous will participate in carrying out this judgment: "And you shall tread down the wicked, for they will be ashes under the soles of your feet, on the day when I act, says the LORD of hosts" (4:3 [3:21 MT]). The Day of the LORD is directly mentioned one more time in 4:5 [3:23 MT], which promises that Elijah will come before the Day to reconcile relationships between the generations (4:6 [3:24 MT]). This will allow the land to escape being utterly exterminated (*herem*).

For Malachi's audience, the Day of the LORD would only be positive if they were in fact faithful to the covenant, as indicated by the dire words in 3:1–5.[55] However, the good news is that Yhwh himself will initiate the cleansing necessary for his people to be restored. As one scholar states "As before, what returning, seeking, fearing, considering, and guarding does not do will be accomplished by the day of the LORD. Regardless of the people's choice, the LORD

---

54. Boloje and Groenewald, "Day of Yahweh," 72.
55. Boloje and Groenewald, "Day of Yahweh," 76.

will remove sin and restore the humble of the land to their rightful place in Zion."[56]

VIEWING THE BIG PICTURE

Walking through the different presentations of the Day of the LORD throughout the Book of the Twelve above might lead some to despair about being able to salvage a stable concept out of the whole. Some readers might identify with the scholar who states:

> The Day of YHWH motif in the book of the Twelve shows no consistent perspective that enables it to be identified as a redactional principle introduced into the individual twelve books that would unite them into one.... Joel understands the Day of YHWH to be a day of judgment against those who threaten Jerusalem; Amos understands it as a day of judgment against those in Israel who defy YHWH's expectations for social justice; Obadiah understands it as a day of judgment against the nations, beginning with Edom, that destroyed Jerusalem; ... Zephaniah understands it as a day of judgment against those in Jerusalem and Judah who abandon YHWH's expectations; ... Zechariah understands it as a day of judgment against the nations; and Malachi understands it as a day of judgment against those in Judah who reject YHWH's Torah and a day of restoration for those who observe it. In each case, the Day of YHWH motif is tailored to the particular concerns of the individual books in which it appears.[57]

---

56. House, "Endings as New Beginnings," 337.
57. Sweeney, "Isaiah and the Twelve," 105.

However, even though the Day of the LORD can seem to be positive or negative, and can be directed at either Judah or Judah's enemies, all of the depictions of the Day of the LORD in the Twelve share an enduring constant: YHWH *will intervene*. YHWH's "intervention" will be experienced as blessing or punishment based on the obedience of the audience. As a result, the overall effect reminds the listeners of "the necessity of responding appropriately."[58]

Read in canonical order, the contours emerge as follows. Joel begins with judgement for Jerusalem but ultimately describes a future time of the restoration of covenant blessings. Thus, Joel sets the stage for the reader's expectations in the rest of the Twelve. Amos focuses mostly on the aspect of judgment for Israel, but does hint that there will be restoration after this time of purging. Obadiah uses some "day" language for past events, but ultimately promises punishment for the nations and restoration of both kingdoms. Zephaniah increases the tension by describing inevitable worldwide judgement, but nonetheless ends in renewal for Jerusalem. Zechariah gives more details of the component parts of the nations attacking Jerusalem, judgement of the nations, and restoration of Israel, focusing on the implications for the temple. Finally, Malachi reminds his audience that Judah still requires purification to be in relationship with YHWH. Malachi finishes the Twelve by promising that Judah will be involved in judging the nations, but will also require a visit from Elijah to avoid being wiped out themselves.

Surveying this succinct account, one is struck by a point similar to the one that emerged in this book's previous chapter on the theme of "Return." Although the people are unable to make themselves ready of their own effort, YHWH himself, through the Day of the LORD, will

58. Barker, "Day of the Lord," 139.

provide the cleansing necessary to renew his relationship with his people.

CONCLUSION

As we have seen, the theme of the "Day of the Lord" in the Twelve is complicated. Our criteria of specifically locating the use of the word "day" with a future aspect in relation to Yhwh's action has provided us with an expansive and complex picture of the Day of the Lord in the Twelve. But as we have noted above, this picture does have an "enduring constant": Yhwh will intervene with blessing and judgement and do what his people could not do for themselves. He will cleanse them and restore them. This helps us as we read the New Testament authors' use of these Old Testament passages. As in the Old Testament, in the New, we see a twin presence of judgement and restoration that comes through Jesus and through the presence of the Holy Spirit on Pentecost. Jesus's first coming to the world provides us with a picture of God's "enduring constant": God's ultimate intervention in the form of God with us, the Emmanuel, Jesus Christ, God in flesh. Jesus's life, ministry, death, and resurrection and the subsequent giving of the Holy Spirit initiate the Day of the Lord in an important way that Peter describes in his sermon in Acts 2.[59] Yet other New Testament passages that we have surveyed above show how this initial coming of the Day of the Lord was only the first step towards a future Day when the Lord will ultimately judge and restore all things. Among biblical scholars, this idea of the Day of the Lord in two parts is often referred to as "already-not yet" eschatology or "inaugurated eschatology."[60]

59. Hays, *Echoes of Scripture in the Gospels*, 220–21.
60. See Wright, *The Day the Revolution Began*. A precursor of this viewpoint was the "realized eschatology" of C. H. Dodd, in which

THE BOOK OF THE TWELVE

In this New Testament vision of the Day of the Lord, we see the implications of the complex picture of the Day of the Lord in the Twelve playing out in new ways in light of Christ in his first and second coming. For this reason, this chapter has moved from a close reading of the Day of the Lord in the Twelve to these final implications for the Day of the Lord in the New Testament rather than trying to read this the other way around. Using this direction of interpretation allows us to see God's developing plans of intervention for his people and for the world and provides a clearer picture of the complex idea of the Day of the Lord for both the Old and New Testament.

REFLECTION QUESTIONS:

1. What makes a discussion of the "Day of the Lord" so complicated?

2. How have you learned about the "Day of the Lord" in the past? How does starting with the Old Testament (and specifically the Twelve)'s depiction of the Day of the Lord help you better understand the concept?

3. What do you notice about the Day of the Lord in the New Testament based on learning about the picture in the Book of the Twelve?

---

the expected "end times" events were entirely fulfilled in the earthly ministry of Jesus. See Erickson, *Christian Theology*, 1165.

6

CREATION, NATURE, AND LAND

INTRODUCTION

REFERENCES TO THE NATURAL world abound in the Book of the Twelve. Yhwh's gift of the "land" is an essential part of the storyline of the Old Testament. When that land is lost in the exile, God's people are devastated. Regaining the land in the post-exilic era solves some of Israel's problems, but does not meet all of their grand expectations or fulfill all of God's promises. Besides this story of the land, authors of the Twelve are also interested in the physical health of the ground, the plants, and the animals in and beyond Israel's boundaries. In fact, the Twelve uses creation imagery in a wide variety of ways. This chapter will provide an overview of some of these places that nature shows up in the Twelve, using the categories of (1) health of the land as indicator of divine favor, (2) themes of creation and uncreation in the Twelve, (3) celestial imagery in the Twelve, (4) animal imagery in the Twelve, and (5) ecological readings of the Twelve. This exploration will show the broad ways the themes of creation, nature, and land flow with key theological perspectives throughout the Twelve.

THE HEALTH OF THE LAND AS INDICATOR OF DIVINE FAVOR

One of the most common uses of creation imagery in the Twelve relates to fertility and provision as signs of favor contrasted with infertility and lack as signs of judgment. Since this theme is so ubiquitous, we will explore only a few selected examples to show how this imagery works. One early expression of this is in Hos 2:8–9 [2:10–11 MT]: "She did not know that it was I who gave her the grain, the wine, and the oil, and who lavished upon her silver and gold that they used for Baal. Therefore I will take back my grain in its time, and my wine in its season; and I will take away my wool and my flax, which were to cover her nakedness." Here, Hosea uses the image of Israel as Yhwh's wife, a wife who adulterously thanks idols rather than Yhwh for the blessings of fruitful crops. The Israelites were guilty of performing rituals to foreign gods, thinking that these tangible rituals would guarantee them bountiful harvests. Since fertility is commonly associated with feminine bodies in the ancient world, femininity can be a metaphor for the land, and metaphors about women's bodies can be used for fertility rituals.[1] In Hos 2, Yhwh consequently retaliates by retracting the gifts he had previously given to his bride. As one scholar states, "The agricultural bounty of the land is a gift of God; it has been sown by God so to speak. As such, God can take it

---

1. Stovell, "I Will Make Her Like a Desert," 40, 52.

back as an act of judgment."[2] Yhwh demonstrates his ownership of the fruits of the ground by revoking them when his people are unfaithful to him.

Many readers will wonder, however, if this image of Yhwh comes off as overly harsh. Is Yhwh acting like an abusive husband? This calls for careful attention to what the metaphor precisely intends to convey. This punishment should be read as referencing the agricultural image, *not* the marriage image. It should call to mind the covenantal curses of Deut 28:15–68, in which disobedience leads to crop failure and poverty, among other punishments. As Brittany Kim explains: "the stripping of Yhwh's wife is not a gratuitous punishment intended merely to shame her but an object lesson designed to teach her that her lovers are not providing her with fruitfulness like she thought."[3] In other words, Yhwh's love for Israel is so great that he will use any means necessary to draw Israel back to himself. This intended response of Israel's return is spelled out in Hos 2:7b [2:9b MT]: "Then she shall say, 'I will go and return to my first husband, for it was better with me then than now.'"

Nonetheless, Yhwh can likewise return the blessings when his covenant people repent. This promise is extended near the end of Hosea, in 14:6–7 [14:7–8 MT]: "His shoots shall spread out; his beauty shall be like the olive tree, and his fragrance like that of Lebanon. They shall again live beneath my shadow, they shall flourish as a garden; they shall blossom like the vine, their fragrance shall be like the wine of Lebanon." Here, Israel itself is compared to a lush garden that Yhwh will bless if his people turn from their idols and disobedience.[4]

---

2. Braaten, "God Sows," 109.
3. Kim, "How Can I Give You Up," 82–83.
4. Nogalski, "Recurring Themes in the Book of the Twelve," 129.

The book of Joel also uses this theme. The punishment of the locust swarm and the command to repent are the main focus of Joel 1:2—2:17, but the restoration that finally occurs when the people return is again largely centered around the health of the land. Joel 2:18 connects Yhwh's compassion for his people directly with their ground, stating "Then the Lord became jealous for his land, and had pity on his people." This attention to the renewal of the natural world even involves Yhwh directly addressing it, as in 2:21a "Do not fear, O soil," and 2:22: "Do not fear, you animals of the field, for the pastures of the wilderness are green; the tree bears its fruit, the fig tree and vine give their full yield."[5] Here Yhwh speaks to the soil and the animals themselves, promising them comfort and demonstrating their importance to him.

The utilization of this theme in the post-exilic period should be noted as well. Zechariah 8:9–12 connects the gift of fruitful crops to the community's obedience to the command to build the temple. Yhwh promises to rescue the people from the lean years experienced shortly after the return (see Hag 1:6, 10–11) with the description of abundance in Zech 8:12: "For there shall be a sowing of peace; the vine shall yield its fruit, the ground shall give its produce, and the skies shall give their dew; and I will cause the remnant of this people to possess all these things." Although the temple is not yet finished, Zechariah reminds the people that Yhwh will bless them if they follow this command, and this blessing is explicitly described through the fecundity of the land itself.[6]

Finally, the book of Malachi notes that, even after the temple is complete, Yhwh still needs to withhold agricultural prosperity to punish the people's unfaithfulness. In Mal

5. Braaten, "God Sows," 127.
6. Boda, *Haggai, Zechariah*, 383–84.

3:8–10, the people disobey by failing to pay their tithes and offerings.[7] However, once again, if the people have a change of heart and obey, Y<small>HWH</small> will bless their land.[8] Malachi 3:11 states it this way: "I will rebuke the locust for you, so that it will not destroy the produce of your soil; and your vine in the field shall not be barren, says the L<small>ORD</small> of hosts." This theme returns in the warning in the very last verse of the book. After promising the generational transformation effected by Elijah, Mal 4:6b explains the potential consequence: "so that I will not come and strike the land with a curse." This possibility of Y<small>HWH</small> punishing the land in the future draws the reading back to the very beginning of the Twelve, where Hos 1:2b charges that "the land commits great whoredom by forsaking the L<small>ORD</small>." This has the effect of "framing" the Twelve with warnings of the need for covenant faithfulness, and the close connection of the wellbeing of the land with the people's obedience.[9]

For a society entirely dependent on agriculture for sustenance and livelihood, the ability of Y<small>HWH</small> to revoke the fertility of the ground as punishment would have been a powerful incentive to obedience. At the same time, the challenge of maintaining a sole allegiance to Y<small>HWH</small> was considerable in a context where other deities promised much more tangible rituals for ensuring the prosperity of one's crops. In the next section, we will zoom the camera out a bit, and instead of looking specifically at the fertility of the ground, we will consider imagery related to the ultimate origin of the land—creation itself.

---

7. Nogalski, "Recurring Themes in the Book of the Twelve," 129–30.

8. Braaten, "God Sows," 128–29.

9. Braaten, "God Sows," 105.

CREATION AND UNCREATION IN THE TWELVE

The Twelve frequently uses creative references to the creation accounts in Genesis to symbolize an ultimate kind of disorder—the chaos arising from creation itself being undone. Such references to creation move beyond simply discussing the land alone to discussing all the facets of creation, including the land and its plant life, animal life, and humans. Zephaniah 1:2–3 is a good example of this: "I will utterly sweep away everything from the face of the earth, says the LORD. I will sweep away humans and animals; I will sweep away the birds of the air and the fish of the sea. I will make the wicked stumble. I will cut off humanity from the face of the earth, says the LORD." Significantly, the parties that YHWH promises to "sweep away" in v. 3 are listed in the opposite order of their creation in Gen 1: humans (1:26), animals (1:24), birds (1:20b), and fish (1:20a). This is not merely judgment, but an unwinding of the foundational acts of creation. In light of this dramatic image, the violation of the promise made after the flood to never again "cut off" humanity (Gen 9:11, 15) in Zeph 1:3b almost seems like an afterthought.[10]

Zephaniah makes a similar move again in 2:14, when specifically predicting the devastation of Nineveh: "Herds shall lie down in it, every wild animal; the desert owl and the screech owl shall lodge on its capitals; the owl shall hoot at the window, the raven croak on the threshold; for its cedar work will be laid bare." This description of animals resting on "capitals," "window," and "threshold" does more than suggest an abandoned city—it overturns the usual order in which humans are expected to domesticate and have dominion over the animal world.[11] This reminds

---

10. De Roche, "Zephaniah I 2–3," 106.
11. Clark, "Reversing Genesis," 168.

the reader of the expression in Gen 1:26, "let them have dominion," referring to humanity's role in overseeing the non-human creation. This passage in Zephaniah, then, reverses the very boundary between humans and animals established at the beginning of Scripture.[12]

When readers reach the end of Zephaniah in Zeph 3, they will find promises to restore Judah. At a surface level this seems to introduce a contradiction, as the threats of utter devastation given in chs. 1 and 2 were apparently empty. Does this mean that they were "mere" rhetoric and lacking in force? Not at all. Rather, this is a way for "the prophet implicitly to articulate the undeserved mercy of God."[13] The "un-creation" language in chs. 1–2 tells us what the people deserve. The fact that these oracles did not literally take place points to a God who is merciful and gracious, not arbitrary.[14]

It is also worthwhile to examine the function of creation language in its ancient Near Eastern context. The resonances to creation imagery elsewhere (particularly Isa 42:5 and Ps 104:2) are clear in Zech 12:1, as it states, "Thus says the Lord, who stretched out the heavens and founded the earth and formed the human spirit within." In a Persian context, this would have directly challenged the ideology of Persian religion. For example, one text claims that Ahuramazda created the world, established peace for humanity, and made Darius the great king.[15] Not only does Zech 12 assert to the contrary that Yhwh alone is the creator, but in vv. 3 and 6 it describes Jerusalem and Judah as

---

12. Clark, "Reversing Genesis," 169.
13. Clark, "Reversing Genesis," 169.
14. Clark, "Reversing Genesis," 169.
15. Mitchell, "Creation Formula," 305.

devouring the other nations, which challenges the claim of universal peace in the Persian ideology.[16]

Yhwh's threat of undoing creation is arresting and striking. It forces readers to consider the scenario of losing all the structure and stability that they have been familiar with. One important part of creation is the heavens, and the next section will focus specifically on images related to the disturbance of the cosmos itself.

CELESTIAL IMAGERY IN THE TWELVE

One particular facet of the natural world that appears in the prophetic corpus is the array of heavenly bodies, the natural objects visible in the sky. The prophets describe events that were so shocking and far-reaching in their impact that nothing less than the disruption and dislocation of the sun, moon, and stars could suffice as imagery for them.

Joel 2:10 gives the first significant occurrence of the heavens being disturbed in the Twelve. After describing the way the locusts cause devastation for the land, the prophet states "The earth quakes before them, the heavens tremble. The sun and the moon are darkened, and the stars withdraw their shining." While the purpose of this passage is unpacking the "Day of the Lord," which we have already examined in chapter 5, here it is crucial to note that Joel 2's picture of the disturbance of the sun, moon, and stars draws on an older tradition in the Old Testament. In passages like Judg 5:4–5, Yhwh is pictured as the divine warrior defeating all enemy forces that threaten the wellbeing of the entire world. This shaking of the heavens occurs in Joel 2 because the nations, in attacking Jerusalem, are threatening the entire order that Yhwh maintains throughout his cosmos. This imagery comes full circle in Joel 3:15–16a [4:15–16a MT]

16. Mitchell, "Creation Formula," 306, 308.

as the heavens once again become darkened and are shaken as Yhwh emerges to fight for his people: "The sun and the moon are darkened, and the stars withdraw their shining. The Lord roars from Zion, and utters his voice from Jerusalem, and the heavens and the earth shake." Yhwh's salvation of his people involves his lordship over not just the land of Israel, but the entire cosmos.[17]

Since readers who move through the Twelve in order will read Joel immediately before Amos, this imagery of the earth shaking or quaking in Joel 2:10 and 3:16 [4:16 MT] informs similar motifs in Amos. Amos also speaks about the earth shaking. He prophesied two years before a major earthquake (Amos 1:1), and he witnesses Yhwh shaking the thresholds in the temple (9:1). Elsewhere he describes buildings and cities experiencing devastating effects like that of earthquakes (3:15; 6:11; 9:5).[18] Most notably, while describing the sins of Israel and promising punishment, Yhwh states in 8:8: "Shall not the land tremble on this account, and everyone mourn who lives in it, and all of it rise like the Nile, and be tossed about and sink again, like the Nile of Egypt?" This threat is immediately followed by a description of the darkening of the sun (8:9). Taken in connection with the divine warrior tradition from Judg 5:4–5 noted above, Amos uses concepts that remind the reader of Yhwh's salvation of his people and instead uses those motifs to threaten the people with Yhwh's wrath.[19] When read in the context of the cosmic disturbances in Joel (which includes earthquakes), a new layer of significance emerges. The earthquakes in Amos are not merely pointing to Yhwh's immediate judgment on the northern kingdom of Israel that took place in the Assyrian exile, but they also foreshadow the disturbance of the

17. Simkins, "God, History, and the Natural World," 450.
18. Lessing, "Amos's Earthquake," 244.
19. Lessing, "Amos's Earthquake," 244.

entire cosmos as Yhwh emerges to permanently establish his people in his world.[20]

Nahum 1:5 also includes this phenomenon: "The mountains quake before him, and the hills melt; the earth heaves before him, the world and all who live in it." Nahum prophesied about a century after Amos, and, whereas Amos had predicted Yhwh's use of Assyria to punish Israel, Nahum spoke of Yhwh's use of Babylon to punish Assyria. Nonetheless, the promise of a shaking earth in Nah 1:5 draws the reader's attention again to the finality of the Day of the Lord in Joel. Nahum is not merely describing the destruction of Assyria in isolation, but is drawing this event into the realm of imagery of Yhwh's final defeat of all evil, when his kingship will be fully inaugurated.[21]

Haggai 2:6–7 gives the next instance of this earthquake imagery: "For thus says the Lord of hosts: Once again, in a little while, I will shake the heavens and the earth and the sea and the dry land; and I will shake all the nations, so that the treasure of all nations shall come, and I will fill this house with splendor, says the Lord of hosts." In contrast to the contexts of deliverance from military invasion or punishment that we have seen above, in Hag 2 the shaking of the heavens and earth relates to the blessing of the temple rebuilt by the postexilic community. Through rebuilding of the temple, Yhwh's puts the cosmos into right order.[22] Haggai again returns to this earthquake imagery in 2:21, "Speak to Zerubbabel, governor of Judah, saying, I am about to shake the heavens and the earth." This is immediately followed by promises to overthrow the nations (2:22) and make Zerubbabel like a signet ring (2:23). Once again, while the immediate promises here point to proper operation of

20. Lessing, "Amos's Earthquake," 255.

21. Lessing, "Amos's Earthquake," 255.

22. Lessing, "Amos's Earthquake," 256.

the temple worship and a Davidic ruler, these items are part of a much larger whole, and are closely connected to the operations of the entirety of the heavens.[23]

Finally, Zech 14:5 deliberately invokes Amos's earthquake as part of detailing the final battle in which Yhwh rescues his people from their enemies: "And you shall flee by the valley of the Lord's mountain, for the valley between the mountains shall reach to Azal; and you shall flee as you fled from the earthquake in the days of King Uzziah of Judah. Then the Lord my God will come, and all the holy ones with him." The earthquake texts we have looked at previously in the Twelve make it clear that earthquakes are associated with Yhwh appearing in power. Zechariah's vision ends with holiness attributed to the common vessels of the temple (14:20–21),[24] and even "the bells of the horses" (14:20), a surprising development for a ritually unclean animal (Lev 11:1–8). This lends another dimension to the fulfilment of Yhwh's ordering of the cosmos: the spreading of purity even outside of the traditional temple hierarchy.[25]

Thus, the Twelve is full of these pictures of the shaking of the heavens and earth. While these images are rooted in the ancient tradition of Yhwh fighting for his people, it is successively employed for different concrete historical circumstances. Furthermore, when viewed through the "gateway" of the use of this imagery in Joel, it serves to continuously prompt the reader to associate each act of judgment or deliverance in the present with Yhwh's eventual restoration of the entire cosmos. Of course, use of such imagery in the New Testament in passages like Rev 6:12–14 has led many to interpret these passages as literal descriptions of the physical destruction of the planets and bodies

23. Lessing, "Amos's Earthquake," 256.
24. Lessing, "Amos's Earthquake," 257.
25. Boda, *Haggai, Zechariah*, 528.

surrounding the earth, but starting with careful attention to the immediate purpose of these metaphors in their Old Testament contexts can help to give greater clarity to our interpretations of these biblical passages.

While Yhwh's infinite power and might give him the ability to perform awe-inspiring deeds such as shaking the heavens, he simultaneously pays attention to the most minute details of the earthly world as well. The next section will explore some of the animal imagery in the Twelve, and help us consider ways in which the non-human world helps us understand Yhwh and his plan of redemption.

ANIMAL IMAGERY IN THE TWELVE

Although it is difficult to determine if the locusts of Joel 1–2 are in fact real animals or merely symbolic of a foreign army, other places in the Twelve use locusts metaphorically to describe punishment via military force. In its pronouncement of the judgment of Assyria, Nah 3 both refers to Babylon as a devouring locust ("it will devour you like the locust," 3:15a) and refers to the vulnerability of Assyria using locusts ("multiply yourselves like the locust," 3:15b; "your scribes [are] like swarms of locusts settling on the fences on a cold day," 3:17a).[26] It is easy to miss the reference in Hab 1:9b, "with faces pressing forward," unless one notices that some other English versions render this as "hordes" (NIV) or "horde of faces" (NASB). Translated in this way, the invading Babylonian army is compared to a swarm of locusts.[27] Also, when Malachi promises blessing in return for faithful tithing, Yhwh states in 3:11 "I will rebuke the locust for you, so that it will not destroy

26. Nogalski, "Recurring Themes in the Book of the Twelve," 128–29.

27. Nogalski, "Recurring Themes in the Book of the Twelve," 129.

the produce of your soil," in which "the locust" most likely relates to the Persians.[28]

Another key example of animal imagery in the Twelve is the depiction of Yhwh as a lion. This metaphor is used in various ways in the book of Hosea. Hosea 5:14 states "For I will be like a lion to Ephraim, and like a young lion to the house of Judah. I myself will tear and go away; I will carry off, and no one shall rescue." This places Yhwh in opposition to his people and emphasizes his sheer power and ferocity in executing judgment upon them.[29] Later, in Hos 13:7–8, Hosea reinforces this image by placing it in parallel with comparison of Yhwh to a leopard and a bear: "I will become like a lion to them, like a leopard I will lurk beside the way. I will fall upon them like a bear robbed of her cubs, . . . there I will devour them like a lion." This combination of metaphors reminds the reader that Yhwh cannot be simplistically reduced to one tangible image, no matter how powerful or frightening that image is.[30] It also creates a literary effect in which Hosea communicates Yhwh's utter might by drawing the reader's attention to the fact that no single image can accurately encapsulate or communicate it.[31]

Hosea 11:10 uses this metaphor of Yhwh as lion in a positive way. In the midst of an exposition of Yhwh's compassion and love for his people (11:8–9), v. 10 states "They shall go after the Lord, who roars like a lion; when he roars, his children shall come trembling from the west." Although the people are clearly "trembling" in fear, Yhwh nonetheless gathers his people, and they return to their land (11:11). Although Yhwh uses his strength to fight for his people and punish their enemies, they nonetheless

28. Nogalski, "Recurring Themes in the Book of the Twelve," 129.
29. Strawn, *What Is Stronger Than a Lion?* 58–59.
30. Strawn, *What Is Stronger Than a Lion?* 271.
31. Strawn, *What Is Stronger Than a Lion?* 272.

correctly maintain a healthy respect for him, as they have also experienced his wrath being turned against them.[32]

The fact that the authors of the Twelve needed to use animal metaphors to help us understand Yhwh should alert us to the fact that the creatures found in the natural world are important and worthy of our attention. The next section will look at some of the ways the Book of the Twelve can guide us in properly caring for Yhwh's gift of creation.

ECOLOGICAL READINGS OF THE TWELVE

Recent attention to the environmental crises around the globe has led to new ways of interpreting the Bible. While at the simplest level this could include attention to surface-level statements about Yhwh's mandate for humans to care for the natural world, this also involve interpretive lenses that look for the earth being treated as a character with human-like feelings and responses, as well as a tendency to see humanity, plants, and animals as part of tightly related whole, as opposed to the common assumption of a strict division between the human and the non-human.[33] We will explore some examples of these insights applied to Hosea and Joel below.

Hosea 4:3 provides a helpful starting place for exploring this reading strategy: "Therefore the land mourns, and all who live in it languish; together with the wild animals and the birds of the air, even the fish of the sea are perishing." This report occurs immediately after Yhwh outlines the sins of the people in 4:1b–2. While it is easy to dismiss an expression such as "the land mourns" as being "merely" metaphorical, closer consideration shows that the earth here

---

32. Strawn, *What Is Stronger Than a Lion?* 63–64. See also King, "God Is a Lion."

33. Habel and Trudinger, "Preface," vii.

has a voice and is used by Yhwh to deliver his message. Even more notably, this "suffering" of the earth leads directly to the devastation of the plants and the animals, itself a means of bringing judgment against Israel.[34] This indicates that society and the ecological order are bound together much more closely than we might often realize. The word "therefore" at the beginning of v. 3 points back to the list of sins that precede it, which means that societal upheaval causes corruption in the natural world too.[35] It also tells us that this connection exists because of the "moral order" deliberately crafted by Yhwh's design.[36] In other words, Yhwh did not just create raw material. Both human and nonhuman creation have an intrinsic purpose, and they both suffer when one experiences trouble.

Joel is another place in the Twelve that invites such reflections. In the description of the locust plague that opens the book, two of the key attributes of this disaster are an invasion (whether by human army or literal locusts) and agricultural devastation, as seen in 1:6a, "For a nation has invaded my land, powerful and innumerable," and 1:10a, "The fields are devastated, the ground mourns." Readers who are familiar with the book of Deuteronomy will recognize both punishments as signs of consequences of disobedience to the covenant (see Deut 28:38–40, 49–51).[37] However, another way of viewing this would be to understand the covenant as involving Yhwh, the people, and the earth itself, rather than just the former two parties. We see this in Gen 9:17: the "covenant that I [Yhwh] have established between me and *all flesh that is on the earth.*" As a result, the emergency situation in Joel involves

34. Loya, "Therefore the Earth Mourns," 57.
35. Loya, "Therefore the Earth Mourns," 61.
36. Loya, "Therefore the Earth Mourns," 61.
37. Bergmann, "Ecological Appropriation of Joel," 41.

the relationship between humanity and creation itself, not merely humanity and Yhwh.[38] In light of this emphasis on humanity's culpability towards the earth, the commands throughout Joel 1 take on a new significance. The audience is ordered to "Hear this . . . give ear" (v. 2), "Wake up, you drunkards, and weep; and wail" (v. 5), "Lament" (v. 8), and "Be dismayed, you farmers, wail, you vinedressers" (v. 11). If these actions were directed towards current environmental issues, application could include paying more attention to ecological problems today, repenting from shallow materialism and exploitation of nature, and allowing oneself to be emotionally moved by the precarious state of the created world.[39] The use of these powerful calls by Joel shows us that a gut-level reflection is necessary for motivating action rather than simple intellectual awareness.[40]

It is also possible to find significant characterization of the earth itself in Joel 1. The command to "lament" in v. 8 is in the feminine singular in the Hebrew, as compared to the commands of vv. 2 and 5, which are in the masculine plural. This opens the possibility that the command in v. 8 is directed to the earth itself, an interpretation supported by the statement that "the ground mourns" in v. 10.[41] This "mourning" by the ground in v. 10 means that the natural world obeys the commands to grieve before humanity does. Another instance of this phenomenon is in v. 13, where the priests are commanded to lament due to the supply of offerings being extinguished. Read carefully, this teaches us that the institution of temple worship itself depends on the health of the natural world.[42] Finally, the first-person out-

38. Bergmann, "Ecological Appropriation of Joel," 42.
39. Bergmann, "Ecological Appropriation of Joel," 42.
40. Bergmann, "Ecological Appropriation of Joel," 43.
41. Braaten, "Earth Community," 117.
42. Braaten, "Earth Community," 118.

burst in v. 19, "To you, O Lord, I cry," could conceivably be spoken by the earth itself, since the complaint earlier in this chapter was entirely about the sphere of creation. Read in this way, readers can experience the earth calling out to Yhwh for deliverance.[43]

In a postindustrial society, it is easy to become sheltered from the condition of the plants and animals around us. If we understand these living beings as having the capacities for communication and affective response like us, it is easier to not only treat them with proper respect but also to understand just how dependent our physical and spiritual lives are on the condition of the natural world.

VIEWING THE BIG PICTURE

How do the different approaches to ecological themes in the Twelve explored above help us better understand the theology of the Twelve? How do they contribute to our understanding of Yhwh's relationship to the land, the skies, the animals, and the plants? Yhwh asks his people for exclusive faith. Israel needed to look to Yhwh alone to provide bountiful harvests, rather than following the rituals of other gods who seemingly offered more certain results. However, Yhwh's providence and watchful care is not merely over his people and their land. It extends to the entire earth and the heavens as well. When taken in isolation, this phenomenon sounds quite benevolent (and possibly idyllic), instead the exercise of Yhwh's immense power has the effect of disturbing the cosmos as a whole. Yet, these occurrences of cosmic disturbance in times of judgment help us anticipate a final time when Yhwh will put creation in its proper order. Aside from this, the animal world is important as a source of analogies to help us better understand

43. Braaten, "Earth Community," 119.

other realities, including world empires and even aspects of Yhwh himself. But creation is more than a source of illustrations. The Twelve prompts its readers to regard the natural world as having feelings and affective responses to not only its treatment by humanity but also to the state of humanity's relationship with Yhwh.

What more concise conclusions can be drawn from the summary above? Yhwh is sovereign over nature and acts within it in many different ways. Yhwh requires his people to not only look to him for provision, but also to respect and care for nature as his gift, and as an important participant in his covenant.

CONCLUSION

This chapter has provided a survey of five different ways that nature imagery is used in the Book of the Twelve. The first three categories related directly to Yhwh's provision of covenant blessings, and maintenance and restoration of the cosmos as part of fulfilling those blessings. The fourth (animal imagery) noted how creation can help us better understand who Yhwh is. Finally, the last category reminded us that we are dependent on the health of creation, and that the livelihood of plants and animals is not unconnected from our obedience. These explorations thus help us appreciate that in the theology of the Twelve, Yhwh's people are called to not only respect Yhwh's control over nature, but also to properly take care of Yhwh's gift of the land as part of their obedience to him.

REFLECTION QUESTIONS:

1. In the Twelve, how is the relationship between the land itself and the people who live in it depicted?

Creation, Nature, and Land

2. What aspects of celestial or animal imagery in the Twelve surprised or interested you? Why?

3. In what way does an ecological approach to reading the Twelve change your ways of thinking of human beings in relationship to nature?

7

THEODICY AND HOPE

INTRODUCTION

"Where is God in the midst of our suffering and loss?" God's people ask this question in a variety of ways throughout the Book of the Twelve. Beside this question are the equally important questions: "How will God bring justice to our situation?" and "Where is hope?" Questions about human suffering and divine justice fall under a category often termed "theodicy," coming from the Greek words "*theos*," meaning God, and "*dikē*," meaning "justice." While "theodicy" as a formal term in philosophy was developed in the 1700s by G. W. Leibniz, the key elements of "theodicy" existed long before the formal term.[1] Theodicy addresses the idea of "one God, who 'represents goodness and justice,' who 'has power in this world' in which

1. For more on the philosophical idea of theodicy and how it relates to the Book of the Twelve and other prophetic literature, see Athas et al., eds., *Theodicy and Hope in the Book of the Twelve*.

'suffering and evil are a reality.'"[2] Theodicy asks questions about how God responds to suffering and evil, and this inevitably leads to questions about where hope exists in the midst of these difficult circumstances. J. Christiaan Beker argues that, in the biblical story, suffering and hope are not opposing forces, but instead he sees them as intimately and irrevocably linked to one another. God's desire throughout the Bible is to show how suffering can be redeemed and how God can bring hope in the midst of suffering.[3] It should not be surprising then that, in the Twelve, theodicy and hope sit so closely beside one another.

In some ways, theodicy and hope integrate many of the other themes of the Book of the Twelve that we have already explored. When one of God's people asks about theodicy and hope, the answers may come by way of God's interaction with the land, his creation, and the natural world (chapter 6), with a promise of the coming Day of the LORD (chapter 5), with a call for repentance and return (chapter 4), or with a picture of restoration of kingship, whether human or divine (chapter 3), or some combination of each of these other themes. This is why some scholars see theodicy and hope as an integrating theme in the Book of the Twelve that works closely alongside these other themes.[4] The Twelve spans a variety of different difficult historical circumstances that give rise to questions about theodicy and hope, including imperial conquest by the Assyrians, Babylonians, and Persians, the violence of war and destruction of the Jewish temple, the loss of Jewish rulers with foreign rulers put in

2. This is a summary of the explanation by Antti Laato and Johannes C. de Moor in Laato and de Moor, "Introduction," xx. Beth Stovell and Daniel Timmer use this summary in "Introduction," 8.

3. Beker, *Suffering and Hope*.

4. Nogalski, "Recurring Themes in the Book of the Twelve," 125–36.

their place, the painful experience of the exile, and the lack of a full return and fulfilment of all of the expected promises when some of the Israelites are finally able to return to their land under Persian rule. Despite the diversity of specific circumstances of loss and suffering depicted in the books within the Twelve, the Twelve as a whole does tell an overarching story of the hope of God's justice enacted against Israel's enemies and the expectation of God's presence, rule, and restoration. While this story is found throughout the Twelve, this chapter will focus on key books in the Twelve that develop this story: Hosea, Joel, Amos, Micah, Nahum, Habakkuk, Zechariah, and Malachi.

HOSEA

Unlike Habakkuk, which contains direct accusations against God, as we will see below, Hosea does not indict God for his actions. Instead, the thrust of Hosea focuses on how God's judgment against the people of Israel is "just retribution for Israel's sin, emphasizing that the punishment fits the crime."[5] We see this in Hosea's depiction of the passive and active judgments by God against Israel, such as God's removal of protection, allowing Assyria to "devour [their] strength" (7:9). This punishment includes judgments on the land itself, as we saw in chapter 6. For example, Hos 8:7 describes how "the standing grain has no heads, it shall yield no meal" and Hos 4:3 speaks of how "the land mourns, and all who live in it languish, together with the wild animals and the birds of the air, even the fish of the sea are perishing" in this depiction of uncreation. God's active judgment includes God taking back the creation he made by revoking "my bread and my water, my wool and my flax, my oil and my drink" (2:5).

5. Kim, "'How Can I Give You Up, Ephraim?'" 67.

Theodicy and Hope

Yet these passive and active judgments are responses to Israel's sin. As Brittany Kim explains: "Not only does the book employ a rich vocabulary of words from the semantic field of sin, but it also gives considerable space to describing the many ways Israel is at fault. Most significantly, Yhwh declares in 8:1 that the people 'have transgressed my covenant and rebelled against my instruction' (cf. 6:7; 8:12)."[6] Israel's transgression against God's covenant and their active rebellion against God has violated the promises they made to God. The descriptions of these sins in Hosea builds on specific language related to curses in Deuteronomy that lead to the exile and are intended to bring repentance.[7] The theme of idolatry exemplifies this rebellion repeatedly in Hosea. As Hos 10 shows, Israel has built altars and pillars to other gods, worshiping "the calf of Beth-aven," and alongside this they have "plowed wickedness," "reaped injustice," and "eaten the fruit of lies" (10:13). In light of this, Hosea shows that God's judgment, whether active or passive, is justified.

To promote sympathy with his readers, Hosea depicts Yhwh's character through depicting him metaphorically "as an aggrieved husband and rejected parent."[8] Hosea 2–3 pictures Yhwh as a husband whose wife, Israel, has betrayed him and taken other lovers. This picture allows readers to feel the impact of Israel's sin in new ways. Not only has God's wife rejected him, but so have her children, born through their mother's adultery and continuing their mother's idolatrous ways (Hos 2:4–5; 3:1; 4:12–14). Using this metaphor moves the covenantal language into the realm of

---

6. Kim notes the use of a wide range of Hebrew words for sin translated in English as "sin," "iniquity," "evil," "wickedness," and "rebellion." Kim, "'How Can I Give You Up, Ephraim?'" 72n22.

7. Petterson, "Exile and Re-Exile in the Twelve," 46.

8. Kim, "'How Can I Give You Up, Ephraim?'" 67.

the marriage covenant, shifting the picture of Israel's breaking this covenant from rebellion against God as a ruling king to adultery against God as a loving husband and rebellion against God as a loving parent.[9] In doing so, this evokes a sense of sympathy with the reader and a sense of shame in Israel, seeing themselves in these painful images. Yet this form of metaphorical theodicy is also met with metaphorical hope in Hosea. The restoration of God's covenantal relationship with Israel is also pictured metaphorically with the renewal of marriage vows; as God "speak[s] tenderly to her" wooing her back, Israel remembers her love and returns to him (Hos 2:14–15 [2:16–17 MT]).

Hosea adds to the picture of theodicy and hope in the Twelve by showing that "the ultimate aim of Yʜᴡʜ's judgment is to serve as discipline leading the people to repentance and resulting in their restoration to a life of abundant flourishing."[10] Hope in Hosea is intertwined with the language of return and restoration as Israel's metaphorical children are given new names: "not my people" is changed to "my people" (Hos 1:10—2:1 [2:1–3 MT] and 2:22–23 [2:24–25 MT]). Not only are God's people restored, but the land, which once felt God's judgment, is pictured as flourishing: "God will answer and sow the land by bringing back the people and granting them bountiful agricultural products (2:22–23)."[11] The final picture of hope in Hos 14 explicitly uses the language of return, *shuv*, picturing the restoration of love between Israel and God[12] and the hope of the restoration of the land itself using images of "dew," "blossom," "root," "shoots," and "an evergreen cypress" (Hos 14:5–8). In this way, Hosea's picture of theodicy and hope

9. Kim, "'How Can I Give You Up, Ephraim?'" 77–80.
10. Kim, "'How Can I Give You Up, Ephraim?'" 67.
11. Ko, "Theodicy and Hope in the Book of the Twelve," 32.
12. Petterson, "Exile and Re-Exile in the Twelve," 47.

integrates the themes of repentance and return discussed in chapter 4 and judgment and restoration of the land discussed in chapter 6.

JOEL

Joel's depictions of theodicy and hope are interwoven with several other themes in the Twelve including: (1) the purification of the priesthood (Joel 1:13), also found in Malachi, which we will discuss below, (2) the call to lament as part of the people's repentance and return to the LORD (Joel 2:12–14),[13] and (3) the picture of the locust swarm in judgement against Israel (Joel 1:4) and in the promise of God's repayment and restoration of the land (Joel 2:25).[14] All these three themes link additionally to the ultimate "Day of the LORD" depictions in Joel 1–3 [1–4 MT] leading to Joel's picture of God's spirit poured out equally among all of his children.

Regarding the purification of the priesthood, Joel 1:13 provides a picture of lamentations by the priests as a response to God's removal of the land's fertility: "Put on sackcloth and lament, you priests, and mourn, you ministers of the altar, . . . for the grain offering and drink offering are withheld from the house of your God." In a similar vein, Joel 2:17 calls out: "Between the vestibule and the altar, let the priests, the ministers of the LORD, weep." They are encouraged to ask God to spare his people. This action occurs so that it will not be said "among the peoples, 'Where is their God?'" Here the salvation of the people is intertwined

13. Athas, "The Failure of Davidic Hope?" 244–45.

14. Scholars have also explored another form of theodicy in God's judgment against the nations as a means of hope for God's people in Joel 3:4–8 [4:4–8 MT]. See Thomas, "Hope through Human Trafficking?" 88–110.

with the repentance of the priests and their purification.[15] It also points to questions of theodicy ("where is their God?") as a motivating factor in the priest's lament. The hope in these sections is built on notions of return and allusions to God's character displayed in Exod 34:6, similar to Hosea, but with Joel's own flair. In Joel 2:12, the people are encouraged to "return to me with all your heart, with fasting and with weeping and with mourning." Their lamentation and their return are thus linked actions. Joel 2:13 continues using Exod 34:6 to point to God's covenant graciousness to his people: "Return to the LORD your God, for he is gracious and merciful, slow to anger and abounding in steadfast love, and relents from punishing."

This covenant response from God is in turn associated with the locust swarm, another factor in developing both theodicy and hope in Joel. On the one hand, the locust swarm is part of God's just punishment of his people because of their sin as we see from the start of Joel in Joel 1:2–5. On the other hand, in Joel God shows his graciousness to his people by repaying them for the loss that has come from this punishment. As Joel 2:25 describes, the LORD will "repay you for the years that the swarming locust has eaten, the hopper, the destroyer, and the cutter, my great army, which I sent against you." In place of destruction, the LORD sends "abundant rain" and "threshing floors will be full of grain, the vats shall overflow with wine and oil" (Joel 2:24). Thus, in Joel, God overturns what was once a means of destruction and replaces this with hope. Thus, theodicy and hope in Joel use a common image, the locust swarm, to convey God's power over the natural world and his character of justice and mercy.

Shortly after these pictures of the purification and lament of the priests and the overturning of the destruction

---

15. Athas, "The Failure of Davidic Hope?" 244–46.

of the locust swarm comes Joel's picture of the Day of the LORD in 2:28–32 [3:1–5 MT]. The Day of the LORD uses celestial language to picture God's renewal and the outpouring of God's spirit on all people. Joel 2:28–29 [3:1–2 MT] pictures it thus: "Then afterward, I will pour out my spirit on all flesh; your sons and your daughters shall prophesy, your old men shall dream dreams, and your young men shall see visions. Even on the male and female slaves, in those days, I will pour out my spirit." In this way, Joel's vision of hope has a universal function that extends to all peoples—young and old, male and female, free and slave—providing a picture of the hope of God's spirit that points to equality.[16] Thus, Joel's theodicy and hope builds on the imagery of return and restoration discussed in chapter 4, pictured in the Day of the LORD discussed in chapter 5, the celestial and animal imagery discussed in chapter 6, and adds to a vision of theodicy and hope in the Twelve through God's spirit available in the future to *all* of God's people.

AMOS

In Amos, theodicy takes a form that might be more easily called "anthropodicy" or a study of human (*anthropo-*) justice (*-dicy*), a study of the character of human beings. Instead of exploring how a just God could allow for suffering, Amos explores the shocking tendency of human beings to inflict suffering on each other and on the world around them and how God responds to this.[17] This exploration becomes tense because Amos is not speaking only about how external people such as foreign nations have hurt the kingdoms of Israel and Judah, but how these kingdoms have hurt *themselves*

16. For more on equality in the giving of the spirit and its value, see Saracco, "I Will Pour out My Spirit on All People," 268–77.

17. Mak, "The Lawlessness of the Lion-God," 111–40.

through acts of injustice, oppression, and violence against their own people. Furthermore, it is not only external enemies who are the target of YHWH's critique—so too are Israel and Judah. Amos 2's laments against Israel and Judah include the following reasons for the Lord's anger (among many others): "because they sell the righteous for silver, and the needy for a pair of sandals—they who trample the head of the poor into the dust of the earth, and push the afflicted out of the way; father and son go in to the same girl, so that my holy name is profaned" (Amos 2:6). Here we see mistreatment of the poor and the oppressed for the sake of greed as well as sexual immorality as part of the unrighteous acts of Israel. In Amos, God responds to this injustice with the cleansing of the Day of the Lord in Amos 5 and 8 and with the promise of God's "rais[ing] up of the booth of David that is fallen" and the restoration to the land in Amos 9 as we see in chapter 3 and chapter 5 of this book. Thus, judgment and restoration form responses to the questions of theodicy and hope in Amos.

MICAH

Micah's view of theodicy and hope is largely framed by Micah's context amidst Assyrian attack. Yet the subsequent placement of Micah as part of the Twelve also encourages readers to read it in light of Joel and Malachi's conceptions of repentance and purification as part of their answers to questions of theodicy and responses of hope. Micah poses the question of whether God's judgment against all of Judah and Israel should include the innocent among them or whether this judgment goes beyond the sins they have committed.[18] In Micah, a series of catchwords depict the movement from judgment to salvation, providing pictures

18. See Kessler, "Theodicy in Micah," 141–56.

of theodicy and of hope. We can see examples of this in the judgment against Samaria and Jerusalem in Mic 1:2—2:11 followed by the promise of deliverance in Mic 2:12–13 and in God's future purge in 5:10–14 [9–13 MT] followed by the hope of future deliverance in 5:15 [5:14 MT].[19]

Micah 1 begins with pictures of destruction, which are likely a depiction of the Assyrian attack against Jerusalem in 701 BCE. In response to this scene, Micah laments and wails in language similar to Joel's call to lamentations of priests, but adds additional animal imagery to intensify his description: "For this I will lament and wail; I will go barefoot and naked; I will make lamentation like the jackals, and mourning like the ostriches" (Mic 1:8). Like Hosea and Habakkuk, Micah uses the language of "exile" to describe the consequences of Israel and Judah's idolatry (Mic 1:15–16).[20] Micah joins exilic language with the imagery of childbirth. The loss of Zion's king is compared "to the pain of a woman in labour (4:9)—a terrible crisis where there is 'a mixture of pain and fear causing wave-like trembling in the person affected.'"[21] Further Zion's peoples' forced deportation causes writhing and groaning compared to "a woman in labor" (4:10). Petterson states:

> While childbirth, like exile, could potentially end in death (as was common in the ancient Near East), in this case God's punishment does not end in death, but rescue. In Mic. 5:2 (5:3 Eng.) "childbirth is applied as a sign that pain and suffering can lead to new life." Exile

---

19. Ko, "Theodicy and Hope in the Book of the Twelve," 34–35. Ko follows Leslie Allen on the idea of catchwords. See Allen, *The Books of Joel, Obadiah, and Micah*, 260.

20. Petterson, "Exile and Re-Exile in the Twelve," 51.

21. Petterson, "Exile and Re-Exile in the Twelve," 52. Petterson cites Bergmann, *Childbirth*, 110.

is abandonment by Yahweh, until a son is born and the "remnant" of his brothers return—the nation is reunited. The son is the future ideal Davidic king.[22]

Thus, both theodicy and hope in Micah are explored through exile and childbirth imagery. Additionally, like Joel and Hosea, Mic 7:18–19 paraphrases Exod 34:6–7 to speak of God's faithfulness and steadfast love to his people as part of the final pictures of hope and return, *shuv*, in Micah. In this way, Micah builds on hopes of the Davidic monarchy (chapter 3), repentance and return (chapter 4), and animal imagery (chapter 6) to depict theodicy and hope. To this, Micah adds the imagery of childbirth, providing a new avenue for understanding.

NAHUM

Like Amos, Nahum points to the source of human suffering in human beings themselves. Nahum can sometimes be a difficult book for modern readers because of its picture of God's wrath and its call for God to do violence against Nineveh, the capital of Assyria. As Nah 1:2–3 states: "A jealous and avenging God is the LORD, the LORD is avenging and wrathful; the LORD takes vengeance on his adversaries and rages against his enemies. The LORD is slow to anger but great in power, and the LORD will by no means clear the guilty." Nahum's questions of theodicy and his view of hope are directly related to this picture of God as avenging and the call for violence; Nahum pictures hope, in part, as God's ultimate justice against Israel's enemies.

---

22. Petterson, "Exile and Re-Exile in the Twelve," 52. Petterson cites Bergmann, *Childbirth*, 111 for the quotation and cites Goswell, "Davidic Rule in the Prophecy of Micah," 153–56 for his final sentence.

Theodicy and Hope

It is helpful to read Nahum's call in its original context and as part of a larger trajectory related to foreign nations in the Twelve. When Assyria attacked the northern kingdom of Israel, its brutality was immense and created lasting trauma for the Israelite people. Assyria was an imperial superpower attacking the smaller and weaker nation of Israel. Assyria was particularly known for its brutality. Nahum 3:1–3 demonstrates the intense greed and violence of Nineveh: "Ah! City of bloodshed, utterly deceitful, full of booty—no end to the plunder! . . . Horsemen charging, flashing sword and glittering spear, piles of dead, heaps of corpses, dead bodies without end—they stumble over the bodies!" Nahum's description matches with Assyrian statues that show Assyria's enemies impaled naked on stakes, piles of enemies' heads at the feet of two of Sennacherib's scribes, and the dismembered bodies of Assyria's victims with heads, hands, and feet littering the ground.[23] Against this grotesque violence, Nah 1's avenging God is a comforter for the traumatized.[24] Nahum describes God's hope not only in avenging the evil Assyria has done, but also in showing mercy to his people: "For the LORD is restoring the majesty of Jacob, as well as the majesty of Israel" (Nah 2:2 [2:3 MT]).[25] This fits with a larger trajectory in the Twelve we discussed in chapter 3, the hope of the restoration of the nation of Israel and God's return to them. The language in Nah 2 of restoration uses the word *shuv* to describe God's "return" of the majesty of Jacob and Israel. Nahum pictures God's justice amidst the evil violence of Assyria through

23. Belibtreu, "Grisly Assyrian Record of Torture and Death," 51–61.

24. Spronk, "The Avenging God of Nahum as Comforter of the Traumatized," 237–50.

25. Timmer, "'Ah, Assyria Is No More!'" 157–72.

his judgment against Nineveh and pictures God's hope as a form of return and restoration.[26]

HABAKKUK

Of all the books within the Twelve, scholars have most extensively explored Habakkuk's picture of theodicy.[27] This comes in part because of how obviously Hab 1–2 questions God directly about theodicy and hope and because of Habakkuk's original situation during the Babylonian exile. Almost from the very first words, Habakkuk cries to the LORD and accuses the LORD of not hearing and not acting: "O LORD, how long shall I cry for help, and you will not listen? Or cry to you 'Violence!' and you will not save?" (Hab 1:2). Habakkuk describes the dire nature of the situation speaking of "destruction and violence" and "strife and contention" around him (1:3) where "the law becomes slack and justice never prevails. The wicked surround the righteous—therefore judgment comes forth perverted" (1:4). God's law given to promote goodness and the justice intended to come from it seem to be conquered by the wicked. They pervert justice by surrounding the righteous. Human beings have inflicted violence on others, specifically on God's people, and on the land itself; Habakkuk wants to know what God is going to do to change the situation and why God has not *already* acted and saved his people.[28]

As Hab 2 begins, Habakkuk is standing like a watchman (similar to Ezek 3 and 33), awaiting God's response: "I will keep watch to see what he will say to me . . ." (Hab 2:1).

---

26. Petterson, "Exile and Re-Exile in the Twelve," 53.

27. For more on theodicy in Habakkuk, see Ko, *Theodicy in Habakkuk*.

28. Floyd, "The Hope of Habakkuk in the Anthropocene Age," 194–213.

Theodicy and Hope

In this way, Hab 2 initiates a perspective of hope that will continue into Hab 3.[29] Scholars debate whether Habakkuk's questions in Hab 1–2 are judged positively or negatively by God, but Hab 3 ends with a prayer in the form of a song that speaks about God's defense of his people and praises God. Many have argued that Hab 3 was written or added to point to a hopeful response by Habakkuk and in this way to answer Habakkuk's questions in Hab 1–2. Habakkuk 3's judgment against Babylon involves an earthquake described thus: "[The Lord] stopped and shook the earth; he looked and made the nations tremble" (Hab 3:6). The violence Babylon has done against the earth is met with a physical response of the earth shaking (see chapter 6's discussion of earthquakes and divine judgment).[30]

Habakkuk 3 ends with a picture of continued hope amidst struggle: "Though the fig tree does not blossom, and no fruit is on the vines; though the produce of the olive fails, and the fields yield no food; though the flock is cut off from the fold, and there is no herd in the stalls, yet I will rejoice in the Lord; I will exult in the God of my salvation" (Hab 3:17–18). The reason for this continued hope is because of the continued promise of God's strength: "God, the Lord, is my strength; he makes my feet like the feet of a deer, and makes me tread upon the heights" (Hab 3:19). Thus, Habakkuk provides a picture of future hope that is grounded in the power and strength of God, which can cause the future destruction of enemies and cause the prophet (and the people) to rejoice in God as their salvation, even as they currently face desperate and difficult situations.

---

29. Fuller, "The Triumph of Hope in Habakkuk," 173–93.

30. Floyd, "The Hope of Habakkuk in the Anthropocene Age," 194–213.

ZECHARIAH AND MALACHI

When grouping parts of the Twelve, some scholars view Hosea–Zephaniah and Haggai–Malachi as two related groups. Part of the reason for these groupings is historical. Where Hosea–Zephaniah map the experiences of Israel as a nation from Assyrian to Babylonian conquests, Haggai–Malachi explicitly map their experiences under Persian rule after the return from the Babylonian exile. Mark Boda argues that Zechariah forms the bridge between these two prophetic groupings and between the late Assyrian and early Persian prophetic periods within the Twelve. Zechariah does this in multiple ways. First, the Twelve overall mentions Assyria more frequently than Babylon. Despite describing in exquisite detail the impacts of Babylonian destruction of the Jerusalem temple and the Babylonian exile, references to Babylon itself remain vague and even missing in places where we might expect them. In Zech 9–14, this takes on a notable climax, describing the return from exile while using references to Assyria and Egypt rather than Babylon. In doing so, Zechariah places an emphasis on themes in the first half of the Twelve, where we see the rise and fall of Assyria, while also bridging these themes to the period of return from the exile.[31]

As "Zephaniah brings closure to the presentation of empire within the first nine books of the Twelve, a presentation that emphasized Assyria/Nineveh and their rise and fall and paralleled that with Judah's/Jerusalem's fate,"[32] Zechariah draws Haggai–Malachi together with Habakkuk and Zephaniah. This leads to Zechariah's second bridging strategy. Zechariah uses two "rhetorical features": (1) three

---

31. Boda, "Creating and Bridging the Gap," 221–22.
32. Boda, "Creating and Bridging the Gap," 222.

"calls to silence" and (2) three "calls to joy."³³ These calls to silence use the Hebrew word *has*, translated "be silent" or "keep silent," with the word "before," along with a reference to Yhwh:

- "But the Lord is in his holy temple; let all the earth *keep silence before him*!" (Hab 2:20)
- "*Be silent before the* Lord *God*! For the day of the Lord is at hand" (Zeph 1:7a)
- "*Be silent*, all people, *before the* Lord; for he has roused himself from his holy dwelling" (Zech 2:13 [2:17 MT])

The "calls to joy" also appear in Zephaniah and Zechariah where they are addressed to "daughter of Zion" with a call to shout, sing, or rejoice in triumph and/or joy:

- "*Sing aloud*, O daughter Zion; *shout*, O Israel! *Rejoice* and exult with all your heart, O daughter Jerusalem!" (Zeph 3:14)
- "*Sing and rejoice*, O daughter Zion! For lo, I will come and dwell in your midst, says the Lord." (Zech 2:10 [2:14 MT])
- "*Rejoice* greatly, O daughter Zion! *Shout aloud*, O daughter Jerusalem!" (Zech 9:9)

As Boda explains, "Both of these sequences extend across the gap observed between Hosea–Zephaniah and Haggai–Malachi. The sequence of 'calls to silence' begins in Habakkuk, crosses to Zephaniah, and ends in Zechariah, while the sequence of 'calls to joy' begins in Zephaniah, crosses into Zech 2, and ends in Zech 9."³⁴

---

33. Boda, "Creating and Bridging the Gap," 221–22.
34. Boda, "Creating and Bridging the Gap," 223.

Alongside these uses of Zechariah as a bridge, Zechariah–Malachi also function as an essential picture of theodicy and hope for the Twelve by way of their depiction of kingship. As we have already discussed in greater detail in chapter 3, Zechariah–Malachi represents a response to the failure to restore a Davidic kingship. Zechariah speaks against Zerubbabel's attempts at power and force saying: "This is the word of the Lord to Zerubbabel: Not by might, nor by power, but by my spirit, says the Lord of hosts" (Zech 4:6).[35] Yet the Twelve does not completely curb the hope of future Davidic restoration despite the crisis with Zerubbabel, and instead Zechariah offers a continued hope regarding Joshua the high priest (Zech 3:6–8).[36]

However, when we get to Malachi, we realize that this hope through the high priest is also problematic because the priesthood itself has been corrupted and defiled. As with Joel and Micah, which speak of the need for purification and specifically with Joel's call to purify the priesthood, Malachi describes how far the defilement of the priesthood has gone, the ways in which the priesthood has failed, and their need for purification. As Athas points out:

> Unlike Hosea and Amos, who lived centuries earlier when the kingdoms of Israel and Judah were still a reality, Malachi directly addresses priests within the post-exilic situation, when there was no local, native kingdom. His condemnation of the priests is, therefore, perhaps the loudest voice in the Book of the Twelve.[37]

Malachi opens by indicting the priests who "despise" the Lord's name (Mal 1:6). Malachi 1:11–12 compares the

---

35. Athas, "The Failure of Davidic Hope?" 235.
36. Athas, "The Failure of Davidic Hope?" 236–41.
37. Athas, "The Failure of Davidic Hope?" 247.

Theodicy and Hope

praise the priests of Jerusalem's temple give to God compared to the nations, and shockingly the nations are honoring God more than God's own priests are! This leads to Mal 3:1–3's depiction of the LORD's messenger who will be "like a refiner's fire" who will "purify the descendants of Levi" (another name for Israel's priests). It is only through this purification that the priests can give offerings that are pleasing to the LORD again (Mal 3:4). This demonstrates that, while the hope of Davidic kingship has not come by way of Zerubbabel or by way of the priests, the Twelve still promises that God will bring this restoration by his own power alongside judgment. Such a view encourages a picture of theodicy alongside hope that closes the Twelve.

Thus, Zechariah–Malachi's view of theodicy and hope provides a necessary bridge within the Twelve, joining the historically disparate prophets before and after the exile to one another, and giving a picture of hope despite the failure of restoration of the Davidic kingship during their time.

VIEWING THE BIG PICTURE

This exploration of theodicy and hope in the Twelve points to some overarching ways that theodicy and hope frequently interweave with the other themes we have explored in the Twelve. Micah, Zechariah, and Malachi explore the hope of the Davidic monarchy as in chapter 3, including the ways in which it has failed. Micah and Malachi are joined by Joel in exploring the need for purification as part of the repentance involved to experience return and restoration. Hosea, Amos, and Nahum also emphasize the need to return to God as part of their response to the judgement upon the nation of Israel and upon the foreign nations as in chapter 4. In Amos, rather than a focus on justifying God's actions, the emphasis is on exploring the actions of human beings in their sinfulness, pointing to the extremity of Israel and Judah's sins. Meanwhile, Nahum offers hope through God's wrath as a means of comforting the traumatized. Hosea creates sympathy for God by depicting him as an aggrieved husband and a rejected parent. Themes associated with the Day of the Lord explored in chapter 5 arise in Joel, Amos, and Micah's depictions of God's judgment and of God's hope. Joel adds to this image God's spirit poured out on all people and Micah uses the imagery of childbirth to point to hope amidst crisis. Metaphors of land, animals, and celestial bodies found in chapter 6 are intertwined with the explorations of theodicy and hope in Hosea, Joel, and Habakkuk. Through this, we can see that the Twelve builds its understanding of theodicy and hope by way of its other themes and also adds to these themes with new engaging metaphors, causing the reader to think more deeply at each step.

Alongside this metaphorical development is another kind of development. As we move from Hosea to Malachi, we can also trace a shift from vengeance against the nations found in books like Nahum to the potential for nations to come to God as we see in Zechariah and finally the nations as even more faithful to God than Israel in Malachi. There is a sense that, while God's character remains the same throughout the Twelve, the vision of God's mercy continues to surprise the readers of the Twelve as it extends in new ways and calls for God's people to respond with a mirroring of this mercy.

CONCLUSION

While the philosophical term "theodicy" is a modern invention, we can see from our analysis of the Twelve that questions of God's justice and God's character in the face of suffering and loss have played a key role in prophetic writings like the Twelve. Alongside explorations of theodicy in the Twelve have been consistent messages of hope. The theme of theodicy and hope rarely stands on its own, but instead functions as an integrating theme, drawing together other themes within the Twelve and acting as a bridge between smaller groupings of the Twelve. With Hab 3:19, these pictures remind us that even when all around us we see despair and loss, even so "God, the LORD, is my strength."

REFLECTION QUESTIONS:

1. Based on your reading, what does "theodicy" mean? How is it related to hope?
2. How do theodicy and hope relate to other themes in the Twelve?
3. Which of the depictions of theodicy and hope in the Twelve did you find particularly compelling or encouraging? Why?
4. Choose 2 books from the Twelve and compare and contrast their depictions of theodicy and hope. What do you notice about the similarities and differences in these two depictions?

8

LITERARY, LINGUISTIC, AND WISDOM APPROACHES TO THE TWELVE

INTRODUCTION

LITERARY, LINGUISTIC, AND WISDOM approaches to the Twelve began in the early to mid-twentieth century, but found their footing in a real way at the end of the century and into the twenty-first century. Marvin Sweeney points to a shift that happened in the study of the Twelve. An older form of study treated the Twelve Prophets as individual prophetic books, but as early as 1921 scholars like Karl Budde began looking at the Twelve as a coherent literary whole. This interest in the Twelve as a unity grew into new theories

Literary, Linguistic, and Wisdom Approaches to the Twelve

developed in the late 1980s and early 1990s and took on new flavors in the 2000s and years following.[1]

The phrase "literary" has two uses in Old Testament studies. An older way of using the term includes approaches that explore the Twelve's layers of editing called "redaction" and the rhetoric associated with these layers. This approach is often more diachronic (coming from *dia* meaning "across" and *chronos* meaning "time") because it explores how the Twelve became the Twelve across time. We will discuss these redactional approaches in more detail in chapter 9. For this chapter, we will be focusing on "literary" approaches that read the Twelve synchronically (coming from *syn*, meaning "together," and *chronos*, meaning "time" i.e., "the same time"). Such literary approaches are similar to linguistic and wisdom approaches because they focus more on the final biblical text we have before us and on what is within the Twelve itself rather than on how it got there across time. These literary approaches will include studies of the "narrative" structure of the Twelve, uses of intertextuality and/or allusion, studies of symbol and metaphor, as well as other forms of literary analysis.

Alongside these literary approaches, this chapter will also explore two other approaches to the Twelve: linguistic and wisdom. Where literary approaches use studies similar to those we find in English literature and other forms of literary studies, linguistic approaches use the methods within the field of linguistics to study the Twelve. Meanwhile wisdom approaches to the Twelve focus on how the Twelve is indebted to the broader wisdom tradition that we find throughout the Old Testament and particularly in books like Proverbs, Ecclesiastes, and Job. Such wisdom approaches often focus on the role of the sages and scribes. Sages are people in the ancient world associated with wisdom and

1. Sweeney, *Form and Intertextuality*, 175–88.

sharing this wisdom to others, while scribes were the ones in charge of writing down these traditions and copying them to make them available throughout time.

This chapter will explore the following questions around literary, linguistic, and wisdom approaches: Who uses these literary, linguistic, and wisdom approaches to the Twelve? How did these approaches develop compared to other approaches to the individual books of the Twelve? What specific kinds of literary, linguistic, and wisdom approaches have scholars suggested? What insights do these literary, linguistic, and wisdom approaches to the Twelve yield? What are the potential drawbacks to these approaches?

LITERARY APPROACHES TO THE TWELVE

Paul House was one of the earliest to use literary theories and apply them to the Twelve in 1990 in his *Unity of the Twelve*.[2] House used a narrative approach that uses the methods to read story to discuss the story of the Twelve. House focused on plot, genre, characterization, and point of view (POV) as way of showing unity between the parts of the Twelve with one another. House's work, while underappreciated at the time of its publication, has provided a helpful direction for many more recent scholars dealing with issues of intertextuality of the Twelve, characterization in the Twelve, the plot of the Twelve, and other related forms of synchronic analysis.

Another leading approach to the Twelve focuses on intertextuality and the Twelve. While scholars debate how the term "intertextuality" should be applied to biblical studies, in its most basic form intertextuality is the study of how

---

2. House, *Unity of the Twelve*.

one text impacts another text.³ This commonly focuses on the way language, themes, and allusions from an earlier author are used by a later author. In biblical studies, this could explore how the Twelve uses Genesis or Isaiah or any other biblical book or how the New Testament uses the Old Testament. Marvin Sweeney has often explored how the Twelve relate to other books in the Old Testament via intertextuality. Sweeney has explored how Micah and Zechariah interact with Isaiah and how Joel draws together other traditions to bring together the Twelve.⁴ Sweeney's approach shows the value of thinking of the Book of the Twelve in terms of mutual relationship among the Twelve, and also mutual impact between the Twelve and Isaiah. Other scholars like Myrto Theocharous and Jennifer Dines have explored intertextuality in the Twelve by examining how the Twelve makes links via language and themes in the Greek translation of the Old Testament, the Septuagint (LXX) compared to the Hebrew version, the Masoretic text (MT).⁵

A third literary approach to Twelve focuses on symbol and metaphor in the Twelve. This approach often bridges between literary and linguistic approaches as some of these approaches use methods associated with literary studies and others use approaches associated with linguistic studies. Recently biblical scholars have often blended more traditional literary approaches to metaphor in the Twelve with cognitive linguistic approaches called Conceptual Metaphor Theory (CMT). In his influential 1980 book *Metaphors We Live By*, George Lakoff (with his co-writer Mark Johnson) explains metaphor as the way human beings make concrete the many

3. For more on the complexities of "intertextuality" as a term, see Porter, *Sacred Tradition*, 1–48.

4. Sweeney, *Form and Intertextuality*, 189–236.

5. Theocharous, *Lexical Dependence and Intertextual Allusion*; Dines, "Verbal and Thematic Links," 355–70.

abstractions within human thought. This allows people to conceive of abstract notions such as love, anger, argument, and the divine. This conception happens when they transfer the characteristics of one concept to another in a process that Lakoff calls "mapping." A typical example from Lakoff of such a conceptual metaphor is LOVE IS A JOURNEY. We can see this metaphor in phrases like "our relationship has hit a dead-end street," "our marriage is stuck," and "where is our relationship headed?" We understand the abstract concept of love through our physical experiences of how journeys work. In this metaphor, lovers are travelers and the events in their relationship is the journey.[6] Biblical scholars have explored how such conceptions develop in the Old Testament.[7] Examples of more extensive studies of symbol and metaphor in the Twelve include the study of the husband-wife metaphor in Hosea,[8] the Divine Warrior metaphor and metaphors for cities as they relate to warfare in the Twelve,[9] divine metaphors in Micah,[10] the extensive symbolism in Zechariah's visions,[11] and the various uses of animal imagery in the Twelve, as discussed in chapter 6.

The value of such literary approaches is extensive. Literary approaches that focus on narrative can demonstrate how the story of the Twelve flows from beginning to end, emphasizing the unity of the Twelve, points of connection between the books within the Twelve, and the structures that draw together the books. Yet these approaches face

6. Lakoff and Johnson, *Metaphors We Live By* as cited in Stovell, "Conceptual Metaphor," forthcoming.

7. Lancaster, "Metaphor Research and the Hebrew Bible," 235–85.

8. Kelle, "Hosea 1–3 in Twentieth-Century Scholarship," 179–216.

9. Kelle, "Wartime Rhetoric," 95–111; O'Brien, *Challenging Prophetic Metaphor*.

10. Cruz, *Who Is Like Yahweh?*

11. Muller-Lopez, "Purifying and Purging," 66–80.

Literary, Linguistic, and Wisdom Approaches to the Twelve

the criticism that alongside these points of connection are points of divergence. For example, contrast the story of Jonah describing Nineveh's repentance with Nahum, which depends on Nineveh's utter violence and lack of repentance as the reason for God's wrath against them. A literary scholar might argue that Nahum shows Nineveh's return to their evil ways and the impact of this choice, but Nahum and Jonah themselves do not tell us which comes first or second. Thus, while literary approaches can helpfully show points of unity, they need to be balanced with explorations of points of disunity.

Literary approaches that focus on intertextuality are valuable because they show how the Twelve builds on the themes already established in the Old Testament. The tricky part of this discussion is related to the timing of each part of the Old Testament. As we discussed in chapter 1 and will discuss in more detail in chapter 9, the Old Testament came together through editing over a long period of time spanning hundreds of years. There are debates about how old any part of the Old Testament is and when different parts of it were available in the final form we have today. This can impact how easy or hard it is to determine whether authors of the Twelve had access to other parts of the Old Testament.

Explorations of symbol and metaphor that we find in literary and linguistic studies are valuable because they provide new ways for understanding the symbolic and metaphorical language that is frequent throughout the Twelve. One of the struggles with studies of symbol and metaphor, however, is rooted in the problem of historical distance. We are very far away from the ancient times when the Twelve was written. This means that sometimes we struggle with how a particular symbol or metaphor worked in their culture compared to our own. Scholars whose work in metaphor/symbol reconstructs conceptions in the ancient context surrounding the biblical prophets help us to avoid anachronism, but arguments about the time period of any specific book in the Twelve can lead to different suggestions for what symbols and metaphors mean. For example, if we think a book should be read primarily against the background of the eighth century BCE, its symbols/metaphors would be related to entirely different cultures and empires in power than they would if we thought the correct background was the sixth century BCE. This can raise questions about how to interpret a specific metaphor or symbol within its biblical book. Yet overall, each of these literary approaches—whether narrative, intertextual, or metaphorical—give us additional access to the meaning and vision of the Twelve.

LINGUISTIC APPROACHES TO THE TWELVE

One could speak of any study of the grammar or language of the Old Testament and the Twelve as "linguistic" because it is focused on the study of language. In this case, we might include comparing words in different languages that are similar to Hebrew or demonstrating when lines are using parallelism as forms of linguistic study. While such approaches to the Twelve specifically have linguistic connections, the "linguistic approaches" we discuss in this chapter are those that build directly on the academic discipline of linguistics.

Early linguistic study of the Twelve developed in the 1970s and 80s and focused on statistical linguistic analysis.[12] More recently linguistic approaches have tended to explore the different stages of developments in Biblical Hebrew to

---

12. Radday and Wickmann, "Unity of Zechariah," 30–55; Portnoy and Petersen, "Biblical Texts," 11–21.

determine the likely dates when parts of the Twelve were written.[13] Another form of linguistics that has influenced the study of the Twelve is systemic functional linguistics (SFL) and its exploration of register and discourse analysis. SFL was developed in the 1970s and 80s by M. A. K. Halliday. Its use in the study of the Twelve did not begin until the twenty-first century with scholars such as Colin Toffelmire on Joel and David Fuller on Habakkuk.[14] Both Toffelmire and Fuller have demonstrated how using SFL can highlight particular themes in parts of the Twelve. For example, Toffelmire's work shows how such studies of discourse and register analysis build on existing approaches to the Twelve, like form criticism, but offer ways to fill existing gaps. In doing so, Toffelmire offers a compelling new way of adding to our understanding of the theme of the Day of the LORD. Similarly, Fuller's work on Habakkuk examines discourse analysis using an SFL lens and highlights the different perspectives of speakers in Habakkuk.

Another area of linguistics that has been used to study the Twelve is textlinguistics, which developed as part of SIL International, an organization that works on biblical translation. The textlinguistics developed by Robert Longacre has been used by scholars such as E. Ray Clendenen to examine discourse analysis in the Twelve within Longacre's genre categories. Clendenen explored the areas of Situation/Indictment, Change/Instruction, Deterrent/Judgment, and Incentive/Salvation in the Twelve.[15]

Finally, some scholars have examined the impacts of speech act theory developed originally by linguists J. L.

13. Young et al., *Linguistic Dating of Biblical Texts*.

14. Toffelmire, *A Discourse and Register Analysis*; Fuller, *A Discourse Analysis of Habakkuk*.

15. Clendenen, "Textlinguistics and Prophecy in the Book of the Twelve," 385–99.

Austin and John Searle. Speech act theory focuses on the linguistic rules around performing different kinds of speech acts such as "resigning, promising, asserting, and asking."[16] Cullen Tanner applied speech act theory to his study of how Revelation uses Zechariah.[17]

Such linguistic approaches offer a wide array of closer examination of how the language of the Twelve demonstrates its rhetorical and theological purposes, its ways of demonstrating the perspectives of speakers, and the social locations of the Twelve. Linguistic approaches offer ways of filling in the gaps and answering common questions in interpretation of the Twelve by way of the linguistic data within the text itself.

WISDOM APPROACHES TO THE TWELVE

Unlike literary and linguistic approaches, which are tied to another discipline (literature and linguistics), wisdom approaches to the Twelve are steeped in the themes of wisdom in the ancient world. As we can see in biblical books like Proverbs and Ecclesiastes, traditionally described as "wisdom literature," wisdom in the ancient world includes several key tenets. First, writings on wisdom focus on wise behavior, wise speech, and being a wise person. This theme of wisdom is commonly contrasted with the actions of the foolish or wicked. As we can see in Prov 1 and Ps 1 (a wisdom psalm), these two directions of wise vs. foolish actions are often depicted as two pathways or roads. The wise are guided by a fear of the LORD, while the foolish despise the LORD and the LORD's laws.[18] Another key characteristic in wisdom literature is an emphasis on the place of wisdom

---

16. *Stanford Encyclopedia of Philosophy*, "Speech Acts."

17. Tanner, "Climbing the Lampstand-Witness-Trees," 81–92.

18. Bartholomew and O'Dowd, *Old Testament Wisdom Literature*.

within God's creation. The picture of God as creator is central to wisdom literature. Often this picture of creation is teamed with pictures of God's temple and explorations of God's role in undoing evil.[19]

In his essay "Where Shall Wisdom be Found in the Book of the Twelve," Daniel Timmer points to other connections between wisdom literature and the Twelve. He compares questions of divine justice and human behavior in Job as a wisdom book and places two books from the Twelve alongside in comparison: Habakkuk and Nahum. Timmer notes how Job and Habakkuk both frame their reflections through speeches directed to God questioning divine justice. Both books find their ultimate resolution in the hope of a future restoration and this hope comes "through the channel of divine revelation, not sapiential reflection."[20] In other words, God himself appears before Job and Habakkuk to answer their questions by revealing something about the nature of God and the nature of the world they inhabit. Neither are given clear wisdom-based answers. Timmer describes these two books as having a "family resemblance."[21] Nahum shares many of these same elements as Job and Habakkuk, but does not use the first-person speech of the prophet in the same way. Thus, Timmer argues that Habakkuk and Nahum share "prominent thematic and semantic features with well-known members of the sapiential family."[22] In other words, these books within the Twelve show they share a family resemblance with wisdom literature through their themes and language.

---

19. Van Leeuwen, "Scribal Wisdom and Theodicy," 31–49; Van Leeuwen, "Cosmos, Temple, House," 399–422.

20. Timmer, "Where Shall Wisdom Be Found," 158.

21. Timmer, "Where Shall Wisdom be Found," 158.

22. Timmer, "Where Shall Wisdom be Found," 163.

Beyond sharing the characteristics of wisdom literature, some recent scholarship by scholars like Jutta Krispenz has argued that the same groups of scribes who copied and shared wisdom literature like Proverbs were also copying and sharing prophetic literature at the same time. If this is the case, we would not be surprised to see similarities between wisdom and prophetic literature emphasized.[23] Groups of scholars, like those writing in the volume *Scribes as Sages and Prophets: Scribal Traditions in Biblical Wisdom Literature and in the Book of the Twelve*, have explored this idea throughout the individual books within the Twelve and in discussing the Twelve as a corpus.[24]

In this way, wisdom approaches to the Twelve can highlight not only the characteristics shared by wisdom literature and the Twelve, but also examine the processes by which we receive these books historically and the impact that process has on similarities between these two traditions.

VIEWING THE BIG PICTURE

Literary, linguistic, and wisdom approaches provide us with different ways of thinking about the Twelve. Each approach also focuses on different parts of the Twelve. Literary approaches can provide an overarching picture of the story the Twelve tells and zoom in on specific details, such as symbol and metaphor. Linguistic approaches can show us the metaphorical, rhetorical, interpersonal, and situational impacts of grammar in the Twelve. Wisdom approaches demonstrate the extensive role of wisdom in prophetic literature and the specific ways the parts of the Twelve show

---

23. Krispenz, ed., *Scribes as Sages and Prophets*.

24. For example, Macintosh explores wisdom traditions in Hosea. See Macintosh, "Hosea and the Wisdom Tradition," 124–32.

this scribal development. Each of these three approaches can lead in turn to thoughtful theological reflection on the Twelve. For example, as Mason Lancaster explores metaphors in Hosea using literary and linguistic approaches, he shows how they together build towards depictions of God. When Raymond Van Leeuwen compares the Twelve to wisdom literature, he highlights the theological themes present in wisdom literature, such as theodicy, that are also found within the Twelve. Similarly, Katrina Larkin's work on wisdom themes in Zechariah explores the eschatology of Zech 9–14.[25] In this way, literary, linguistic, and wisdom approaches can provide helpful connections to the theological approaches we discussed in chapter 2.

REFLECTION QUESTIONS:

1. What are the key features of literary and linguistic approaches to the Twelve?
2. How are the Twelve related to wisdom literature?
3. What are the unique contributions of literary, linguistic, and wisdom approaches to the Twelve?
4. Of the three approaches (literary, linguistic, or wisdom), which do you find most helpful? What makes this approach valuable to you?

---

25. Larkin, *The Eschatology of Second Zechariah*.

9

HOW WAS THE TWELVE WRITTEN AND FORMED?

INTRODUCTION

THUS FAR, THIS BOOK has explored themes in the Twelve and approaches to the Twelve. As our book reaches its conclusion, we finish off where we began: exploring what makes the Twelve "the Twelve." When we talk about the process of creating the Twelve, we can speak of the entire formation or compositional process. This includes the writing process and the editing process (which we also call "redaction"). This chapter examines how the Twelve came to be, how it was written, how it was edited, and the long process that shaped the Twelve into what we have today when we open a Bible.

EVIDENCE OF EDITORIAL WORK

It is common in churches today to think of the Bible in its final form, in the version we find in our NIV or NRSV or NKJV. This approach tends to treat the Bible as though the books we have came to us in this form from the start. For some readers who are used to studying the books of the Bible at "face value," it may initially seem confusing why scholars hypothesize about how these books were written and how they were put together. These readers may ask, "Why couldn't these books simply have been written down in the essential form we have today?" However, there are several good reasons to think that editors who wrote, organized, and expanded the original words of the prophets were also part of the "inspired" process by which the Bible came to be. Scholars sometimes call this editorial activity "redactional" or "redaction". This section will briefly review some of these proposed devices, along with examples.

The first type of editorial device in the Twelve is *superscriptions*, which are typically at the beginning of each book. An example would be Hos 1:1, "The word of the LORD that came to Hosea son of Beeri, in the days of Kings Uzziah, Jotham, Ahaz, and Hezekiah of Judah, and in the days of King Jeroboam son of Joash of Israel." This provides a description of the nature of the book ("the word of the LORD"), the name and family of the prophet ("Hosea son of Beeri"), and the time period of the prophet's ministry (by listing the contemporaneous kings). Other superscriptions give information regarding the subject matter of the book, such as in Nah 1:1: "An oracle concerning Nineveh. The book of the vision of Nahum of Elkosh." Sometimes superscriptions occur in the middle of books rather than at the beginning. Habakkuk 3:1 reads "A prayer of the prophet Habakkuk according to Shigionoth." Based on this, some scholars have posited that Hab 1–2 originally existed independently, and that Hab 3 was a later addition.[1]

Another device similar to a superscription is the *incipit*. The word "incipit" comes from the Latin "here it begins." An incipit goes beyond a simple title and tells a "narrative."[2] This can be seen in both Zech 1:1 and 1:7. Zech 1:1 reads: "In the eighth month, in the second year of Darius, the word of the Lord came to the prophet Zechariah son of Berechiah son of Iddo, saying." Similarly, Zech 1:7 states: "On the twenty-fourth day of the eleventh month, the month of Shebat, in the second year of Darius, the word of the Lord came to the prophet Zechariah son of Berechiah son of Iddo; and Zechariah said . . . ."

As seen in the examples from Zechariah in the paragraph above, some book introductions also contain precise *dates*, which themselves can be a clue to editorial activity. These dating formulas in Zech 1:1, 1:7, and 7:1 are very similar to those throughout the previous book, Haggai. Examples can be seen in Hag 1:1 ("In the second year of King Darius, in the sixth month, on the first day of the month, the word of the Lord came by the prophet Haggai to Zerubbabel son of Shealtiel, governor of Judah, and to Joshua son of Jehozadak, the high priest") and 2:10 ("On the twenty-fourth day of the ninth month, in the second year of Darius, the word of the Lord came by the prophet Haggai, saying") (see also 1:15—2:1 and 2:20). These close time periods and dating formulas have led some scholars to conclude that the same editor revised and organized Haggai and Zechariah 1–8 to function together.[3]

While superscriptions and incipits are ways that editors organized and provided framing expectations for

---

1. Redditt, "Editorial/Redaction Criticism," 172.
2. Redditt, "Editorial/Redaction Criticism," 173.
3. Redditt, "Editorial/Redaction Criticism," 175.

earlier prophetic texts, other types of devices include insertions of similar content to create connections throughout books and collections of books. One such device is *quotations*. The most significant example of linking quotations in the Twelve is the chain of partial quotations of Exod 34:6–7 in Joel 2:13, Jonah 4:2, Mic 7:18, and Nah 1:2–3 (see further discussion of this phenomena throughout chapter 4 above).[4]

Another comparable device is *catchwords*, which sometimes seem to be employed to stitch the end of one book to the beginning of another. Catchwords can involve either multiple words that occur in close proximity to each other, or even whole phrases or sentences that occur at the seams of two adjoining books. As will be seen below, this device is a core part of Nogalski's argument. Readers who compare the final passages of Joel with the beginning of Amos will find a significant parallel between Joel 3:16 [4:16 MT] and Amos 1:2,[5] as seen in the chart below:

Joel 3:16 [4:16 MT]	Amos 1:2
The LORD *roars from Zion, and utters his voice from Jerusalem, and the heavens and the earth shake. But the* LORD *is a refuge for his people, a stronghold for the people of Israel*	*The* LORD *roars from Zion, and utters his voice from Jerusalem; the pastures of the shepherds wither, and the top of Carmel dries up*

Here the parallels consist in the verbatim repetition of the first two clauses, "The LORD roars from Zion, and utters his voice from Jerusalem." So not only are several key words shared between the passages, but they are even placed in the same order.

4. Redditt, "Editorial/Redaction Criticism," 174.
5. Shepherd, "Compositional Analysis," 186.

Several of the earlier chapters of this book have looked at connecting themes across the Book of the Twelve. Given the recurrence of multiple themes throughout, it is not surprising that some scholars have interpreted these *thematic connections* as signs of redaction rather than different prophets merely being interested in similar subject matter. For example, both Joel 1:2—2:17 and Hag 1:6, 10–11 reference agricultural devastation as evidence of Yhwh's judgment on sin.[6] Scholars have also argued for the existence of *structures* that span multiple books. One such proposal is that the theophanies in Nah 1 and Hab 3 deliberately mirror each other, leading some to argue that Nahum and Habakkuk were originally a single composition.[7]

With these examples of editorial devices in mind, the next section will put the pieces together by surveying some of the ways that scholars have used this kind of evidence to come up with theories about how the Twelve was assembled.

MODELS FOR THE REDACTION OF THE BOOK OF THE TWELVE

This section will survey four important proposals that scholars have offered for how the Book of the Twelve was assembled into its current form. The four theories surveyed below were created by scholars named Dale Schneider, James Nogalski, Aaron Schart, and Jakob Wöhrle, respectively.

---

6. Redditt, "Editorial/Redaction Criticism," 174.
7. Redditt, "Editorial/Redaction Criticism," 174–75.

Dale Schneider

In considering the formation of the Twelve, it is important to note one early source that was influential in advancing this area of study.[8] Dale Schneider's 1979 dissertation, "The Unity of the Book of the Twelve," argues that the Twelve began with an initial collection of Hosea, Amos, and Micah, which was drawn together by Hezekiah's court scribes.[9] Next, Nahum, Habakkuk, and Zephaniah was assembled by Josiah, and added to the three earlier books sometime near the end of the exile.[10] A later collection of Joel, Obadiah, and Jonah was also gathered into the Twelve at this time.[11] In the post-exilic period Haggai and Zech 1–8 existed independently before being added to the collection, and Zech 9–14 and Malachi were added to complete the collection in the fifth century.[12] Schneider's proposal is relatively streamlined as compared to the theories that will be outlined below, as it simply deals with the books as a whole, rather than considering the process by which the smaller components of each book were assembled.

Stage	Books
Stage 1	Collection of Hosea, Amos, Micah
Stage 2a	Collection of Nahum, Habakkuk, Zephaniah, added to Hosea, Amos, and Micah

---

8. For a survey of other sources that addressed this topic throughout the nineteenth and mid-twentieth centuries, see Sweeney, "Twelve, Book of the," 790–92.
9. LeCureux, *Thematic Unity*, 7.
10. Sweeney, "Twelve, Book of the," 791.
11. LeCureux, *Thematic Unity*, 8.
12. LeCureux, *Thematic Unity*, 8.

Stage	Books
Stage 2b	Collection of Joel, Obadiah, Jonah, also added to the rest of the Twelve thus far
Stage 3	Haggai and Zech 1–8 added to the Twelve
Stage 4	Zech 9–14 and Malachi added to the Twelve

James Nogalski

Like Schneider, James Nogalski's work is interested in how the Twelve were assembled over time, yet Nogalski's approach is more extensive than Schneider's. In 1993, Nogalski outlined his approach to the redaction of the Book of the Twelve in his two-volume set consisting of *Literary Precursors to the Book of the Twelve* and *Redactional Processes in the Book of the Twelve*. His argument is largely based around catchword links between the various books. For Nogalski, the first collection that led to the Twelve consisted of early editions of Hosea, Amos, Micah, and Zephaniah, which are all united by their Deuteronomistic outlook.[13] These four books also have similar superscriptions, which present a connected chronology:[14]

Hos 1:1	*The word of the* LORD *that came to Hosea son of Beeri, in the days of Kings Uzziah, Jotham, Ahaz, and Hezekiah of Judah, and in the days of King Jeroboam son of Joash of Israel.*

---

13. Redditt, Review of *Literary Precursors*, 105.
14. Nogalski, *Hosea–Jonah*, 5.

Amos 1:1	*The word*s of Amos, who was among the shepherds of Tekoa, which he saw concerning Israel in the days of King Uzziah of Judah and in the days of King Jeroboam son of Joash of Israel, two years before the earthquake.
Mic 1:1	*The word of the* LORD that came to Micah of Moresheth in the days of Kings Jotham, Ahaz, and Hezekiah of Judah, which he saw concerning Samaria and Jerusalem.
Zeph 1:1	*The word of the* LORD that came to Zephaniah son of Cushi son of Gedaliah son of Amariah son of Hezekiah, in the days of King Josiah son of Amon of Judah.

All of these superscriptions (except for Amos) begin with "The word of the LORD," and proceed to list the kings who were reigning during the ministry of each prophet.

Shortly after this time, an initial edition of Haggai and Zech 1–8 was created.[15] These two earlier collections were drawn together with most of the other books (except for Jonah and Zech 9–14) through redactional work that used Joel as a centering point.[16] Nogalski dates Joel to the end of the fifth century, and views this editing process as involving substantial revisions to both the earlier books and to the earlier editions of Obadiah, Nahum, Habakkuk, and Malachi.[17] These revisions served to add links to Joel to the other books. Some examples of these links are called for. Nogalski sees the dramatic descriptions of the day of YHWH in Zeph 1:15 as intentionally referencing Joel 2:2. The two texts can be compared in the chart below:

---

15. O'Brien, Review of *Literary Precursors*, 130.
16. Redditt, Review of *Literary Precursors*, 106.
17. O'Brien, Review of *Literary Precursors*, 130.

Zeph 1:15	Joel 2:2
That day will be a day of wrath, a day of distress and anguish, a day of ruin and devastation, *a day of darkness and gloom, a day of clouds and thick darkness*	*a day of darkness and gloom, a day of clouds and thick darkness*! Like blackness spread upon the mountains a great and powerful army comes; their like has never been from of old, nor will be again after them in ages to come

The language of "day of darkness and gloom" and "a day of clouds and thick darkness" are notable similarities. He also sees Mic 4:3 as pointing to Joel 3:10 [4:10 MT], as it inverts the latter's formula of turning farming implements into weapons:

Mic 4:3	Joel 3:10 [4:10 MT]
He shall judge between many peoples, and shall arbitrate between strong nations far away; they shall *beat their swords into plowshares, and their spears into pruning hooks*; nation shall not lift up sword against nation, neither shall they learn war any more	*Beat your plowshares into swords, and your pruning hooks into spears*; let the weakling say, "I am a warrior"

Finally, according to Nogalski, after 332 BCE, Zech 9–14 and Jonah were added to the Book of the Twelve.[18] Nogalski bases this precise date on the reference to Greece in Zech 9:13.[19] Why does Nogalski single out Zech 9–14 and Jonah as being the last books to enter the collection of

18. Rogers, Review of *Literary Precursors*, 721.
19. O'Brien, Review of *Literary Precursors*, 131.

the Twelve? They are the two lone exceptions to his general observation that catchwords link the end of each book to the beginning of the next one in their order in the Hebrew canon (such as the connection between Joel and Amos documented above). There are no discernible links between Jonah 4 and Mic 1, nor is there any significant vocabulary shared between Zech 14 and Mal 1. However, Nogalski notes that the hymn in Jonah 2, which many scholars believe to be an addition that post-dates the rest of the book, does contain links to Mic 1, and additionally Zech 8 does connect to Mal 1.[20] These connections provide strong evidence of Jonah and Zech 9–14 being the last books to enter the Twelve. Nogalski's understanding of Jonah being added to the Twelve near the end of the process has implications for the significance of the book, as he argues that "Jonah represents Israel as a whole, and the temple [see Jonah 2:4, 7 (2:5, 8 MT)] takes on greater importance."[21]

The chart below will summarize the major steps of Nogalski's proposal for the composition of the Twelve. It is important to note that each stage involved harmonizing editorial work in the books of the previous stages.

Stage	Books
Stage 1	Collection of Hosea, Amos, Micah, and Zephaniah
Stage 2	Collection of Haggai and Zech 1–8
Stage 3	Two collections joined with Joel as centering point, previous books also linked to Joel: Obadiah, Nahum, Habakkuk, and Malachi
Stage 4	Zech 9–14 and Jonah added

20. Rogers, Review of *Literary Precursors*, 720.
21. O'Brien, Review of *Literary Precursors*, 130.

Modern redactional study of the Twelve builds on Nogalski's work. All subsequent studies have either adapted his proposal or have responded to Nogalski's theories in some way. This will become apparent as we explore the theories of Aaron Schart and Jakob Wöhrle in the next two sections.[22]

Aaron Schart

Aaron Schart builds on the work of Nogalski in his 1998 book (written in German), entitled *The Making of the Book of the Twelve Prophets: New Adaptations of Amos as Part of Cross-Script Editing Processes*.[23] Schart finds a secure foundation point in the book of Amos, as Amos was both the earliest prophet in the Twelve and also the first place where many of the key themes in the Twelve appear (as was seen in the thematic chapters of this book).[24] Schart thus starts by analyzing the literary development of Amos in isolation. He then uses the six different compositional layers he detects in Amos as a starting point for determining theologically comparable levels of redaction throughout the rest of the Twelve. Schart argues that the original version of Amos consisted of the superscription in 1:1 along with an early core of the oracles in Amos 3–6.[25] Schart argues that this early core of Amos was combined with an early version of Hosea, due to the similarity of their messages, in the first stage of the development of the Book of the Twelve.[26] This

---

22. Schart, "History of Interpretation," 814.

23. Schart, *Entstehung*. The full German title is *Die Entstehung des Zwölfprophetenbuchs: Neubearbeitungen von Amos im Rahmen schriftenübergreifender Redaktionsprozesse*. The title given in the text above is our English translation.

24. Sweeney, Review of *Entstehung*, 279–80.

25. Lust, Review of *Entstehung*, 178.

26. Sweeney, Review of *Entstehung*, 281.

resulted in the addition of the second superscription in 1:2, along with the words of judgment against the nations in Amos 1–2 and the visions of Amos 7–9.[27]

The second stage of the composition of the Book of the Twelve is what Schart calls the Deuteronomistic Corpus. According to Schart, it incorporated early versions of Micah and Zephaniah, in a manner similar to Nogalski's initial stage of Hosea, Amos, Micah, and Zephaniah, as seen above. The addition of these books involved the writing of Amos 2:4–5, 10–12; 3:1b, 7; 4:6–11; 8:4–7; 9:7–10.[28] As a whole, the themes of this four-book collection include the "Day of Yhwh against Israel . . . [which] is relevant for Judah as well . . . [and] the dtr [Deuteronomistic] concept of centralization in Zion over against Beth El."[29] Another link that unites Hosea, Amos, and Micah specifically is the "summons to hear"[30] which recurs several times in each book. Three examples of this phenomenon are given in the chart below:

Hos 4:1	*Hear* the word of the Lord, *O people of Israel*; for the Lord has an indictment against the inhabitants of the land. There is no faithfulness or loyalty, and no knowledge of God in the land.
Amos 3:1	*Hear* this word that the Lord has spoken against you, *O people of Israel*, against the whole family that I brought up out of the land of Egypt:
Mic 3:1	And I said: *Listen, you heads of Jacob and rulers of the house of Israel!* Should you not know justice?—

The remaining compositional layers in Schart's argument can be covered more succinctly. The third step of

27. Lust, Review of *Entstehung*, 178.
28. Lust, Review of *Entstehung*, 179.
29. Sweeney, Review of *Entstehung*, 282.
30. Redditt, "Formation of the Book of the Twelve," 17.

the redaction of the Twelve happened when Nahum and Habakkuk were added to the earlier four books. The key connection Schart identifies here is between the "hymnic-layer" in Nah 1 and Hab 3 and the "doxologies" of Amos 4:13; 5:8; 9:6.[31] For Schart, the uniting focus of this new six-book collection was "Yhwh's role as universal creator and judge of nations."[32] Stage four involved the integration of Haggai and Zechariah. Schart argues that this layer deals with the theme of "salvation," as "it was felt that Israel's punishment had come to end, and that hope for a better future was justified."[33] This layer corresponds to the insertion of Amos 9:11, 12b, 13a, 14–15.[34] Stage five is "eschatological,"[35] and it brought in Joel and Obadiah, along with Amos 9:12, 13b, and 4:9.[36] This stage sets the earlier writings in the context of the expectation of a "universal day of Yhwh."[37] With the book of Amos now in its full canonical form, Schart's sixth and final layer involves the addition of Malachi and Jonah. For Schart, Jonah "is introduced to provide a view of Yhwh's mercy that critiques Joel and other portrayals of Yhwh's judgment,"[38] while "Malachi is introduced to serve as a conclusion to the Book of the Twelve that builds upon the eschatological perspective of the JOK [Joel–Obadiah corpus] redaction but emphasizes the ethical dimensions of Mosaic Torah and prophecy."[39]

---

31. Lust, Review of *Entstehung*, 179.
32. Sweeney, Review of *Entstehung*, 283.
33. Lust, Review of *Entstehung*, 179.
34. Lust, Review of *Entstehung*, 179.
35. Sweeney, Review of *Entstehung*, 283.
36. Lust, Review of *Entstehung*, 179.
37. Sweeney, Review of *Entstehung*, 283.
38. Sweeney, Review of *Entstehung*, 283.
39. Sweeney, Review of *Entstehung*, 283.

The chart below will summarize the major steps in Schart's proposed development of the redaction of the Twelve. As was the case for Nogalski above, each stage involves the books from the previous stages being edited to fit with their new canonical neighbors.

Stage	Books
Stage 1	Amos and Hosea (early versions)
Stage 2	Deuteronomistic Corpus: Micah and Zephaniah (early versions)
Stage 3	"Hymnic-layer": Nahum and Habakkuk
Stage 4	Salvation layer: Haggai and Zechariah
Stage 5	Eschatological layer: Joel, Obadiah, and final additions to Amos
Stage 6	Malachi and Jonah

Even a cursory summary of Schart's argument reveals significant overlap with Nogalski's proposal. It is particularly noteworthy that they arrived at many similar conclusions, even though Schart's process—of starting with Amos by itself—was quite different. We will explore these similarities and differences in greater depth below. However, there is one more proposal for the composition of the Twelve that must be considered first.

Jakob Wöhrle

Like Schart, Jakob Wöhrle's work is written in German. Like Nogalski and Schart, he is interested in the history of composition for the Twelve, but his methods differ. Jakob Wöhrle's approach to the composition of the Twelve is laid out in his two monographs, *The Early Collections of the*

Book of Twelve Prophets: Genesis and Composition (2006) and *The Conclusion of the Book of the Twelve Prophets: Cross-Book Editing Processes in the Late Collections* (2008).[40] His approach is slightly different than that of Nogalski and Schart, since the core of his argument deals with a posited eight-stage redactional process that starts with significant portions of Amos, Micah, Zephaniah, Haggai, Nahum, Joel, and Zechariah, building the rest of the Twelve through thematic additions that affected the entire corpus. He does, however, address the development of the earlier stages as well.

Wöhrle's "prehistory" of the Twelve begins in a manner similar to Nogalski, with a "Book of the Four" (early versions of Hosea, Amos, Micah, and Zephaniah) existing alongside a combined edition of early versions of Haggai and Zechariah sometime in the early fifth century.[41] In an original twist, however, Wöhrle then argues that Hosea was removed from this collection and replaced with an early version of Joel.[42] For Wöhrle, this placement of Joel at the beginning of the collection "highlights the plight of the people of Israel under the nations and the importance of the 'Day of the Lord,' and it proclaims that the way to salvation is through repentance."[43]

This brings us to the place where Wöhrle's redactional layers of the Twelve begin. The first stage inserted

---

40. Wöhrle, *Die frühen Sammlungen*; Wöhrle, *Abschluss*. Their full German titles are *Die frühen Sammlungen des Zwölfprophetenbuches: Entstehung und Komposition* and *Der Abschluss des Zwölfprophetenbuches: Buchübergreifende Redaktionsprozesse in den späten Sammlungen*, respectively. The titles given in the text above are our English translations.

41. Tiemeyer, Review of *Die frühen Sammlungen*, 373.

42. Tiemeyer, Review of *Die frühen Sammlungen*, 374.

43. Tiemeyer, Review of *Die frühen Sammlungen*, 374.

proclamations of Yhwh's judgment against foreign nations.[44] This material was written at the beginning of the fourth century BCE and represented a turning away from Yhwh's previous judgment upon Judah.[45] The second stage, which was inserted in the middle of the fourth century, deals with the hope of Yhwh raising up a new Davidic ruler who will restore international peace. These texts include Amos 9:11, 12b; Mic 4:8; 5:1–4 [4:14—5:3 MT]; and Zech 9:10.[46] Wöhrle's third level of redaction is another layer focused on foreign nations. This level addressed the nations that were hostile to Judah at the beginning of the third century, and included additions to Joel and Amos. It also resulted in the inclusion of significant parts of Obadiah and Malachi.[47] This collection found its unity in the themes of the "punishment of Edom and the cosmological dimension of the final judgment."[48] Wöhrle's fourth level of redaction brought in Habakkuk, which previously had not been connected to the other books in the Twelve.[49]

The fifth stage of redaction in Wöhrle's model addresses the theme of salvation for foreign nations. This includes texts such as Mic 4:1–4, Obad 17a, and Zech 2:11–12 [15–16 MT].[50] Wöhrle argues that this layer was composed in the early third century, and "was created in response to those Jews who were attracted to the culture and religion of Hellenism."[51] This layer asserts that the nations needed to

44. Weyde, Review of *Abschluss*, 364.

45. Tiemeyer, Review of *Die frühen Sammlungen*, 374.

46. Tiemeyer, Review of *Die frühen Sammlungen*, 374; Weyde, Review of *Abschluss*, 364.

47. Tiemeyer, Review of *Die frühen Sammlungen*, 374.

48. Weyde, Review of *Abschluss*, 364.

49. Weyde, Review of *Abschluss*, 364.

50. Tiemeyer, Review of *Die frühen Sammlungen*, 375.

51. Tiemeyer, Review of *Die frühen Sammlungen*, 375.

be obedient to Yhwh's law, rather than Yhwh's people taking on the beliefs of the nations. Wöhrle's sixth redactional stage dates to the second half of the third century and deals with the theme of grace. This layer involved the insertion of the allusions to Exod 34:6 in Joel 2:13; Jonah 4:2; Mic 7:18–20; Nah 1:2–3; and Mal 1:9. Wöhrle believes these allusions function together to not only provide cohesion for the corpus as a whole, but also assert that "Yhwh's mercy explains the divine willingness to forgive."[52] This was also the stage where Jonah was added to the Twelve.[53]

The seventh layer inserted Mal 4:4–6 [3:22–24 MT]. This created a sense of comprehensiveness for the collection as a whole: the references to the Day of Yhwh link back to Joel, while the occurrence of Moses links back to the book of Joshua, which is the beginning of the collection of the prophets in the Hebrew canon. This leads to the prophets being a major collection that come after Torah, also known as the Pentateuch.[54] Wöhrle's eighth and final redactional level simply involves Hosea being reintegrated into the Twelve, as it was noted above that Hosea had been removed prior to the main eight redactional stages.[55]

Given the complicated nature of Wöhrle's proposal, it is appropriate to summarize it using a chart, as has been done for the previous theories:

---

52. Weyde, Review of *Abschluss*, 365.
53. Tiemeyer, Review of *Die frühen Sammlungen*, 375.
54. Tiemeyer, Review of *Die frühen Sammlungen*, 375.
55. Tiemeyer, Review of *Die frühen Sammlungen*, 375.

How Was the Twelve Written and Formed?

Stage	Books
Stage 0	1. Collection of Hosea, Amos, Micah, and Zephaniah (early versions)
	2. Collection of Haggai and Zechariah (early versions)
	3. Hosea removed from collection 1 and replaced by Joel
Stage 1	Judgment against foreign nations (added to Amos, Micah, Zephaniah, Haggai, Nahum, Joel, and Zechariah)
Stage 2	Hope of a future Davidic king (added to Amos, Micah, and Zechariah)
Stage 3	Further judgement against foreign nations (Obadiah and Malachi; insertions in Joel, Amos, and Zechariah)
Stage 4	Habakkuk added
Stage 5	Salvation for the nations (insertions in Joel, Obadiah, Micah, Zephaniah, Zechariah)
Stage 6	Grace (Jonah; insertions in Joel, Micah, Nahum, Malachi)
Stage 7	Conclusion (Malachi 4:4-6 [3:22-24 MT])
Stage 8	Reintegration of Hosea into the Twelve (Hosea)

Comparison of Redaction Models

Similarities and differences emerge when we compare the models of Nogalski, Schart, and Wöhrle outlined above. All three of these scholars agree that the Twelve began with a "Book of the Four" (Hosea, Amos, Micah, and Zephaniah), although Schart distinguishes an additional earlier collection of just Hosea and Amos. Nogalski and Wöhrle agree that the next step was a combination of Haggai and Zechariah. Nogalski and Wöhrle also agree that Joel was a crucial early work that brought thematic stability to the collection, although Wöhrle sees Joel as entering the Twelve later than Nogalski does. Nogalski and Schart agree that Jonah was one of the last books to be brought into the Twelve, and Wöhrle likewise places Jonah in one of the later layers. For Nogalski and Schart, Nahum and Habakkuk entered at the same time, whereas Wöhrle sees them as separate. The next section will consider some viewpoints that are outside of the redactional paradigm entirely.

ALTERNATIVE PERSPECTIVES

But what if the models sketched out above are wrong? Other scholars see the books within the Twelve as being fully independent compositions rather than parts of a deliberately unified corpus. Ehud Ben Zvi has raised a number of challenges against the various redactional models. Starting with the evidence from the ancient manuscripts of and references to the Twelve reviewed in the introductory chapter in this book, Ben Zvi notes that the Dead Sea Scrolls treat the Twelve as entirely separate prophetic books.[56] Additionally, the fact that the order of the Twelve is different in the Septuagint shows that a very early reading audience did not recognize an intentional or deliberate order to the Twelve.[57] The Septuagint also obscures many of the "catchwords" that Nogalski and others argued were deliberate links between the books. Therefore, according to scholars like Ben Zvi, ancient readers would not have viewed the Twelve as a unified corpus, or, if such an intention was present at the beginning, it was forgotten or abandoned very quickly.[58]

56. Ben Zvi, "Twelve Prophetic Books," 130–34.
57. Ben Zvi, "Twelve Prophetic Books," 134.
58. Ben Zvi, "Twelve Prophetic Books," 134–35.

Ben Zvi is also skeptical of the redactional arguments that involve posited "quotations" or "allusions" between different books in the Twelve, as the Twelve is also highly intertextual with the so-called Major Prophets (Isaiah, Jeremiah, Ezekiel) and even portions of the Old Testament outside the prophets.[59] Therefore to Ben Zvi's mind, the mere presence of similar phrases within the Twelve does not provide convincing evidence that it was intended to be read as a unified whole. Ben Zvi is equally skeptical about the treatment of superscriptions by redactional scholars. For Ben Zvi, superscriptions actually serve to differentiate books from one another, rather than creating continuity or unity between them.[60]

Ben Zvi devotes further attention to what he sees as the weaknesses of arguments based upon catchwords. For example, he cites Nogalski's argument for an original link between the end of Obadiah and the beginning of Micah (since, for Nogalski, Jonah was a later insertion). Nogalski argues that the shared words "mountain," "Jacob," "fire," "Samaria," and "field" found in Obad 15–21 and Mic 1:1–7 are evidence that ancient redactors deliberately connected the two books. Ben Zvi instead notes that all of these words are very common, and that a scholar could easily claim a connection between any two random books by picking and choosing shared words in this way.[61] Ben Zvi concludes his critique by noting some overarching weaknesses of the redactional approaches. One weakness is that the reconstructed editorial layers are highly speculative. Also, it leads to a mode of reading in which immediate literary context is often ignored in favor of implications derived

---

59. Ben Zvi, "Twelve Prophetic Books," 135–37.
60. Ben Zvi, "Twelve Prophetic Books," 137.
61. Ben Zvi, "Twelve Prophetic Books," 140.

from supposed references to other texts.[62] Ben Zvi instead proposes that the books of the Twelve be read as individual, unified, compositions. He states, "the intended readers were more likely to follow textually inscribed markers suggesting a scheme about what the book was about, and about strategies of reading and rereading, rather than to decide that the text was written so as to mislead them, and accordingly, to ignore these discursive and literary markers."[63] This raises a powerful challenge for proponents of the redactional models. Would ancient editors have created a textual conglomerate that could only be properly understood if it was first "taken apart" into its earlier layers?

This section has reviewed some of the counterarguments raised against the redactional models reviewed earlier in this chapter. This raises challenging questions about how the Twelve should be interpreted. Are the arguments for redactional layers based on catchwords and thematic associations as strong as Nogalski and the others claim? The next section will review what has been covered and offer some ways forward.

VIEWING THE BIG PICTURE

This chapter has surveyed the types of evidence that scholars draw upon when attempting to discern what type of editorial activity took place for a given book. These devices included superscriptions, incipits, dates, citations, catchwords, and thematic connections. Next, four proposals were reviewed. Schneider, Nogalski, Schart, and Wöhrle each made use of some or all of the lines of evidence surveyed above to come up with their own models for how the Twelve was assembled. While these models

62. Ben Zvi, "Twelve Prophetic Books," 149.
63. Ben Zvi, "Twelve Prophetic Books," 150.

(particularly those of the latter three) had certain similarities regarding the order in which certain books entered the collection, they had significant differences as well. Finally, we covered some of the arguments against the redactional models. Specifically, Ben Zvi argues that ancient readers did not seem to treat the Twelve as a unified corpus, and that the arguments based on quotations, superscriptions, and catchwords are far from conclusive.

While we may not be fully equipped to decisively declare one particular approach as being clearly superior at this point, this presentation of different perspectives should help us do one thing better: ask the right questions. With these models and arguments in mind, our journey through the biblical text will be far richer. As we read various passages in the Twelve, we can imagine what they might have meant if they were composed in different time periods and how they might have been intended to connect to other texts in different ways. We will be able to read the Twelve as part of an exciting scholarly conversation. As we continue to re-read and internalize its content, we can insightfully reflect on which scholarly approaches make the best sense of the evidence. Our book has worked towards showing the value of reading the Twelve in relation to each other, while offering a diversity of perspectives on this topic to keep these questions alive.

CONCLUSION

In this book, we have explored what it means for the Twelve to be called "the Twelve." We began in chapter 1 by introducing the idea of "the Book of the Twelve" as a grouping of prophetic books that function as unified "Book." In chapter 2, we charted the wide and diverse trajectories of studies of theology in the Twelve. In chapters 3–7, we explored the theological themes that bind the Twelve together: the expectation of the Davidic kingship's restoration and the hope found in God's universal kingship (chapter 3); God's call for the people to repent and return tied to the promise of God's return to his people (chapter 4); the announcements of the Day of the LORD as the day that God intervenes to bless and to judge (chapter 5); the role of all of creation (the land, the heavens, and the animals) in the theological landscape of the Twelve (chapter 6); and the promise of God's justice and hope amidst situations of suffering and loss (chapter 7). In chapters 8–9, we shifted from a thematic approach to the Twelve to examination of the methods used to study the Twelve, whether literary, linguistic, wisdom-oriented (chapter 8), or focused on the compositional history of the Twelve (chapter 9). In this way our final chapter returned to where our book began with the question: What makes the Twelve "the Twelve"? Throughout this journey, we have walked a pathway through the Twelve that shows how reading the Twelve as a unified Book offers new vistas for theological insight with fresh views of God's care for his people, his active participation in the world, and his desire to give hope even in the darkest places.

REFLECTION QUESTIONS:

1. What editorial devices may have been used to draw together different parts of the Twelve?

2. Of the redactional approaches offered by Schneider, Nogalski, Schart, and Wöhrle, which do you find most convincing? Why?

3. What aspects that bind the Twelve together did you find most helpful? What implications does studying the Twelve in this way have for your own life and for the world today?

BIBLIOGRAPHY

Abernethy, Andrew T., and Gregory Goswell. *God's Messiah in the Old Testament: Expectations of a Coming King*. Grand Rapids: Baker, 2020.

Albertz, Rainer. "Exile as Purification: Reconstructing the 'Book of the Four.'" In *Thematic Threads in the Book of the Twelve*, edited by Paul L. Redditt and Aaron Schart, 232–51. BZAW 325. Berlin: de Gruyter, 2003.

Albertz, Rainer, James D. Nogalski, and Jakob Wöhrle, eds. *Perspectives on the Formation of the Book of the Twelve: Methodological Foundations—Redactional Processes—Historical Insights*. BZAW 433. Berlin: de Gruyter, 2012.

Allen, Leslie C. *The Books of Joel, Obadiah, and Micah*. NICOT. Grand Rapids: Eerdmans, 1976.

Andiñach, Pablo R. "Latin American Approaches: A Liberationist Reading of the 'Day of the Lord' Tradition in Joel." In *Method Matters: Essays on the Interpretation of the Hebrew Bible in Honor of David L. Petersen*, edited by Joel M. LeMon and Kent Harold Richards, 423–40. RBS 56. Atlanta: Society of Biblical Literature, 2009.

Athas, George. "The Failure of Davidic Hope? Configuring Theodicy in the Book of the Twelve in Support of a Davidic Kingdom." In *Theodicy and Hope in the Book of the Twelve*, edited by George Athas et al., 226–50. LHBOTS 705. London: Bloomsbury T. & T. Clark, 2021.

Bibliography

Athas, George, Beth M. Stovell, Daniel Timmer, and Colin M. Toffelmire, eds. *Theodicy and Hope in the Book of the Twelve.* LHBOTS 705. London: Bloomsbury T. & T. Clark, 2021.

Bakon, Shimon. "The Day of the Lord." *JBQ* 38.3 (2010) 149–56.

Barker, Joel D. "Day of the Lord." In *Dictionary of the Old Testament Prophets*, edited by Mark J. Boda and J. Gordon McConville, 132–43. Downers Grove, IL: IVP Academic, 2012.

Bartholomew, Craig, and Ryan O'Dowd. *Old Testament Wisdom Literature: A Theological Introduction.* Downers Grove, IL: IVP Academic, 2011.

Beker, Johan Christiaan. *Suffering and Hope: The Biblical Vision and the Human Predicament.* Grand Rapids: Eerdmans, 1994.

Belibtreu, Erika. "Grisly Assyrian Record of Torture and Death." *BAR* 17.1 (1991) 51–61.

Ben Zvi, Ehud. "Twelve Prophetic Books or 'The Twelve': A Few Preliminary Considerations." In *Forming Prophetic Literature: Essays on Isaiah and the Twelve in Honor of John D. W. Watts*, edited by James W. Watts and Paul R. House, 125–56. JSOTSup 235. Sheffield: Sheffield Academic, 1996.

Bergmann, Claudia D. *Childbirth as a Metaphor for Crisis: Evidence from the Ancient Near East, the Hebrew Bible, and 1QH XI, 1–18.* BZAW 382. Berlin: de Gruyter, 2008.

Bergmann, Neil W. "Ecological Appropriation of Joel." *Australian eJournal of Theology* 20.1 (2013) 34–48.

Biddle, Mark E. "Dominion Comes to Jerusalem: An Examination of Developments in the Kingship and Zion Traditions as Reflected in the Book of the Twelve with Particular Attention to Micah 4–5." In *Perspectives on the Formation of the Book of the Twelve: Methodological Foundations—Redactional Processes—Historical Insights*, edited by Rainer Albertz et al., 253–68. BZAW 433. Berlin: de Gruyter, 2012.

Boadt, Lawrence. *Reading the Old Testament: An Introduction.* 2nd ed. New York: Paulist, 2012.

Boda, Mark J. "Creating and Bridging the Gap: Assyria and Babylon in the Presentation of Theodicy and Hope in the Book of the Twelve." In *Theodicy and Hope in the Book of the Twelve*, edited by George Athas et al., 214–25. LHBOTS 705. London: Bloomsbury T. & T. Clark, 2021.

———. "A Deafening Call to Silence: The Rhetorical 'End' of Human Address to the Deity in the Book of the Twelve." In *The New Form Criticism and the Book of the Twelve*, edited by Mark J. Boda et al., 183–204. ANEM 10. Atlanta: Society of Biblical Literature Press, 2015.

———. *Haggai, Zechariah*. NIVAC. Grand Rapids: Zondervan, 2004.
———. "Oil, Crowns and Thrones: Prophet, Priest, and King in Zechariah 1:7—6:15." In *Exploring Zechariah*. Vol. 2. *The Development and Role of Biblical Traditions in Zechariah*, 59–82. ANEM 17. Atlanta: Society of Biblical Literature Press, 2017.
———. *'Return to Me': A Biblical Theology of Repentance*. NSBT 35. Downers Grove, IL: IVP Academic, 2015.
Boda, Mark J., and Michael H. Floyd, eds. *Tradition in Transition: Haggai and Zechariah 1-8 in the Trajectory of Hebrew Theology*. LHBOTS 475. London: T. & T. Clark, 2008.
Boda, Mark J., Michael H. Floyd, and Colin M. Toffelmire, eds. *The Book of the Twelve and the New Form Criticism*. ANEM 10. Atlanta: Society of Biblical Literature Press, 2015.
Boloje, Blessing Onoriode, and Alphonso Groenewald. "Malachi's Eschatological Day of Yahweh: Its Dual Roles of Cultic Restoration and Enactment of Social Justice (Mal 3:1–5; 3:16—4:6)." *OTE* 27 (2014) 53–81.
Bowman, Craig. "Reading the Twelve as One: Hosea 1–3 as an Introduction to the Book of the Twelve (the Minor Prophets)." *Stone-Campbell Journal* 9 (2006) 41–59.
Braaten, Laurie J. "Earth Community in Joel 1–2: A Call to Identify with the Rest of Creation." *HBT* 28.2 (2006) 113–29.
———. "God Sows: Hosea's Land Theme in the Book of the Twelve." In *Thematic Threads in the Book of the Twelve*, edited by Paul L. Redditt and Aaron Schart, 104–32. BZAW 325. Berlin: de Gruyter, 2003.
Bulkeley, Tim. "The Book of Amos and the Day of Yhwh." *Colloq* 45.2 (2013) 154–69.
Clark, David A. R. "Reversing Genesis: A Theological Reading of Creation Undone in Zephaniah." *ExpTim* 123.4 (2012) 166–70.
Clendenen, E. Ray. "Textlinguistics and Prophecy in the Book of the Twelve." *JETS* 46 (2003) 385–99.
Creach, Jerome F. D. *Joshua*. IBC. Louisville, KY: Westminster John Knox, 2011.
Crenshaw, James L. "Theodicy in the Book of the Twelve." In *Thematic Threads in the Book of the Twelve*, edited by Paul L. Redditt and Aaron Schart, 175–91. BZAW 325. Berlin: de Gruyter, 2003.
Cruz, Juan. *Who Is Like Yahweh?: A Study of Divine Metaphors in the Book of Micah*. FRLANT 263. Göttingen: Vandenhoeck & Ruprecht, 2016.
De Roche, Michael. "Zephaniah I 2–3: The 'Sweeping' of Creation." *VT* 30 (1980) 104–9.

De Vries, Simon J. "Futurism in the Pre-exilic Minor Prophets Compared with That of the Postexilic Minor Prophets." In *Thematic Threads in the Book of the Twelve*, edited by Paul L. Redditt and Aaron Schart, 252–72. BZAW 325. Berlin: de Gruyter, 2003.

Delkurt, Holger. "Sin and Atonement in Zechariah's Night Visions." In *Tradition in Transition: Haggai and Zechariah 1-8 in the Trajectory of Hebrew Theology*, edited by Mark J. Boda and Michael H. Floyd, 235–51. LHBOTS 475. London: T. & T. Clark, 2008.

Dines, Jennifer. "Verbal and Thematic Links between the Books of the Twelve in Greek and Their Relevance to the Differing Manuscript Sequences." In *Perspectives on the Formation of the Book of the Twelve: Methodological Foundations—Redactional Processes—Historical Insights*, edited by Rainer Albertz et al., 355–70. BZAW 433. Berlin: de Gruyter, 2012.

Dodd, C. H. *The Apostolic Preaching and Its Development*. Chicago: Willet, Clark, 1937.

Erickson, Millard J. *Christian Theology*. 2nd ed. Grand Rapids: Baker, 1998.

Evans, Craig A. "The Book of the Twelve in Jesus and the New Testament." In *The Book of the Twelve: Composition, Reception, and Interpretation*, edited by Lena-Sofia Tiemeyer and Jakob Wöhrle, 385–414. VTSup 184. Leiden: Brill, 2020.

Floyd, Michael H. "The Hope of Habakkuk in the Anthropocene Age." In *Theodicy and Hope in the Book of the Twelve*, edited by George Athas et al., 194–213. LHBOTS 705. London: Bloomsbury T. & T. Clark, 2021.

Flynn, Shawn W. *YHWH Is King: The Development of Divine Kingship in Ancient Israel*. VTSup 159. Leiden: Brill, 2014.

Fox, Nili S. "Kingship and the State in Ancient Israel." In *Behind the Scenes of the Old Testament: Cultural, Social, and Historical Contexts*, edited by Jonathan S. Greer et al., 475–83. Grand Rapids: Baker, 2018.

Fuller, David J. *A Discourse Analysis of Habakkuk*. SSN 72. Leiden: Brill, 2019.

———. "The Triumph of Hope in Habakkuk." In *Theodicy and Hope in the Book of the Twelve*, edited by George Athas et al., 173–93. LHBOTS 705. London: Bloomsbury T. & T. Clark, 2021.

Gärtner, Judith. "Jerusalem—City of God for Israel and for the Nations in Zeph 3:8, 9–10, 11–13." In *Perspectives on the Formation of the Book of the Twelve: Methodological Foundations—Redactional*

Processes—Historical Insights, edited by Rainer Albertz et al., 269–83. BZAW 433. Berlin: de Gruyter, 2012.

Goswell, Gregory. "David in the Prophecy of Amos." *VT* 61 (2011) 243–57.

———. "'David their King': Kingship in the Prophecy of Hosea." *JSOT* 42 (2017) 213–31.

———. "Davidic Rule in the Prophecy of Micah." *JSOT* 44 (2019) 153–65.

———. "A Theocratic Reading of Zechariah 9:9." *BBR* 26 (2016) 7–19.

Green, Mitchell. "Speech Acts." *The Stanford Encyclopedia of Philosophy* (Fall 2021). Online: https://plato.stanford.edu/archives/fall2021/entries/speech-acts

Grenz, Stanley J. *Theology for the Community of God*. Grand Rapids: Eerdmans, 2000.

Habel, Norman C., and Peter Trudinger. "Preface." In *Exploring Ecological Hermeneutics*, edited by Norman C. Habel and Peter Trudinger, vii–viii. SymS 46. Atlanta: Society of Biblical Literature Press, 2008.

Hays, Richard B. *Echoes of Scripture in the Gospels*. Waco, TX: Baylor University Press, 2016.

Hecke, Pierre van. "Conceptual Blending: A Recent Approach to Metaphor Illustrated with the Pastoral Metaphor in Hos 4:16." In *Metaphor in the Hebrew Bible*, edited by P. van Hecke, 215–32. BETL 187. Leuven: Peeters, 2005.

———. "'For I Will Be like a Lion to Ephraim': Leonine Metaphors in the Twelve Prophets." In *The Book of the Twelve Prophets: Minor Prophets—Major Theologies*, edited by Heinz-Josef Fabry, 387–402. BETL 295. Leuven: Peeters, 2018.

Hoffman, Yair. "The Day of the Lord as a Concept and a Term in the Prophetic Literature." *ZAW* 93 (1981) 37–50.

House, Paul R. "The Character of God in the Book of the Twelve." In *Reading and Hearing the Book of the Twelve*, edited by James D. Nogalski and Marvin A. Sweeney, 125–45. SymS 15. Atlanta: SBL, 2000.

———. "Endings as New Beginnings: Returning to the Lord, the Day of the Lord, and Renewal in the Book of the Twelve." In *Thematic Threads in the Book of the Twelve*, edited by Paul L. Redditt and Aaron Schart, eds., 313–38. BZAW 325. Berlin: de Gruyter, 2003.

———. *The Unity of the Twelve*. JSOTSup 97. BLS 27. Sheffield, UK: Almond, 1990.

Ishai-Rosenboim, Daniella. "Is יוֹם ה' (the Day of the Lord) a Term in Biblical Language?" *Bib* 87 (2006) 395–401.

Jeremias, Jörg. "The Function of the Book of the Joel for Reading the Twelve." In *Perspectives on the Formation of the Book of the Twelve: Methodological Foundations—Redactional Processes—Historical Insights*, edited by Rainer Albertz et al., 77–87. BZAW 433. Berlin: de Gruyter, 2012.

Jerome. *Biblia Sacra Vulgata*. Vol. 2. Stuttgart: Würtembergische Bibelanstalt, 1969.

Jones, Philip. "Divine and Non-Divine Kingship." In *A Companion to the Ancient Near East*, edited by Daniel C. Snell, 243–59. 2nd ed. Blackwell Companions to the Ancient World. Hoboken, NJ: Wiley Blackwell, 2020.

Kelle, Brad E. "Hosea 1–3 in Twentieth-Century Scholarship." *CurBR* 7 (2009) 179–216.

———. *Hosea 2: Metaphor and Rhetoric in Historical Perspective*. AcBib 20. Leiden: Brill, 2005.

———. "Wartime Rhetoric: Prophetic Metaphorization of Cities as Female." In *Writing and Reading War: Rhetoric, Gender, and Ethics in Biblical and Modern Contexts*, edited by Brad E. Kelle and Frank Richard Ames, 95–111. SymS 42. Atlanta: Society of Biblical Literature Press, 2008.

Kessler, Rainer. "Theodicy in Micah." In *Theodicy and Hope in the Book of the Twelve*, edited by George Athas et al., 141–56. LHBOTS 705. London: Bloomsbury T. & T. Clark, 2021.

Kim, Brittany. "'How Can I Give You Up, Ephraim?' (Hosea 11:8a): Theodicy in Hosea." In *Theodicy and Hope in the Book of the Twelve*, edited by George Athas et al., 66–87. LHBOTS 705. London: Bloomsbury T. & T. Clark, 2021.

King, Andrew M. "God Is a Lion: Leonine Imagery in Hosea." *Credo* (May 23, 2018) [n.p.]. Online: https://credomag.com/2018/05/god-is-a-lion-leonine-imagery-in-hosea/

Ko, Grace. "Theodicy and Hope in the Book of the Twelve." In *Theodicy and Hope in the Book of the Twelve*, edited by George Athas et al., 22–39. LHBOTS 705. London: Bloomsbury T. & T. Clark, 2021.

———. *Theodicy in Habakkuk*. Paternoster Theological Monographs. Milton Keynes: Paternoster, 2014.

Krispenz, Jutta, ed. *Scribes as Sages and Prophets: Scribal Traditions in Biblical Wisdom Literature and in the Book of the Twelve*. BZAW 496. Berlin: de Gruyter, 2021.

Laato, Antti, and Johannes C. de Moor. "Introduction." In *Theodicy in the World of the Bible: The Goodness of God and the Problem of Evil*, edited by Antti Laato and Johannes C. de Moor, vii–liv. Leiden: Brill, 2003.

Lakoff, George, and Mark Johnson. *Metaphors We Live By*. Chicago: University of Chicago Press, 1980.

Lancaster, Mason D. "Metaphor Research and the Hebrew Bible." *CurBR* 19 (2021) 235–85.

Larkin, Katrina J. A. *The Eschatology of Second Zechariah: A Study of the Formation of a Mantological Wisdom Anthology*. CBET. Kampen: Kok Pharos, 1994.

LeCureux, Jason T. *The Thematic Unity of the Book of the Twelve*. HBM 41. Sheffield, UK: Sheffield Phoenix, 2012.

Lessing, R. Reed. "Amos's Earthquake in the Book of the Twelve." *CTQ* 74 (2010) 243–59.

Loya, Melissa Tubbs. "'Therefore the Earth Mourns': The Grievance of Earth in Hosea 4:1–3." In *Exploring Ecological Hermeneutics*, edited by Norman C. Habel and Peter Trudinger, 53–62. SymS 46. Atlanta: Society of Biblical Literature Press, 2008.

Lust, Johan. Review of *Die Entstehung des Zwölfprophetenbuchs: Neubearbeitungen von Amos im Rahmen schriftübergreifender Redaktionsprozesse*, by Aaron Schart. *ETL* 74 (1998) 178–79.

Macintosh, A. A. "Hosea and the Wisdom Tradition: Dependence and Independence." In *Wisdom in Ancient Israel: Essays in Honor of J. A. Emerton*, edited by John Day et al., 124–32. Cambridge: Cambridge University Press, 1995.

Mak, Chelsea D. "The Lawlessness of the Lion-God: Theodicy in the Book of Amos." In *Theodicy and Hope in the Book of the Twelve*, edited by George Athas et al., 111–40. LHBOTS 705. London: Bloomsbury T. & T. Clark, 2021.

Mayhue, Richard. "The Prophets' Watchword: Day of the Lord." *Grace Theological Journal* 6.2 (1985) 231–46.

Meyers, Carol L., and Eric M. Meyers. "The Future Fortunes of the House of David: The Evidence of Second Zechariah." In *Fortunate the Eyes That See: Essays in Honor of David Noel Freedman in Celebration of His Seventieth Birthday*, edited by Astrid Beck, 207–22. Grand Rapids: Eerdmans, 1995.

Mitchell, Christine. "A Note on the Creation Formula in Zechariah 12:1–8; Isaiah 42:5–6; and Old Persian Inscriptions." *JBL* 133 (2014) 305–8.

Muller-Lopez, Kathryn. "Purifying and Purging: Body Metaphors in the Visions of Zechariah." *Classical Bulletin* 86.1 (2010) 66–80.

Nogalski, James D. *The Book of the Twelve: Micah–Malachi*. SHBC. Macon, GA: Smyth & Helwys, 2011.

———. "The Day(s) of YHWH in the Book of the Twelve." In *Thematic Threads in the Book of the Twelve*, edited by Paul L. Redditt and Aaron Schart, 192–213. BZAW 325. Berlin: de Gruyter, 2003.

———. *Literary Precursors to the Book of the Twelve*. BZAW 117. Berlin: de Gruyter, 1993.

———. "Reading the Book of the Twelve Theologically." *Int* 61.2 (2007) 115–22.

———. "Recurring Themes in the Book of the Twelve: Creating Points of Contact for a Theological Reading." *Int* 61.2 (2007) 125–36.

———. *Redactional Processes in the Book of the Twelve*. BZAW 118. Berlin: de Gruyter, 1993.

Nogalski, James D., and Marvin A. Sweeney, eds. *Reading and Hearing the Book of the Twelve*. SymS 15. Atlanta: Society of Biblical Literature Press, 2000.

O'Brien, Julia M. *Challenging Prophetic Metaphor: Theology and Ideology in the Prophets*. Louisville, KY: Westminster John Knox, 2008.

———. Review of *Literary Precursors to the Book of the Twelve*, by James D. Nogalski and *Redactional Processes in the Book of the Twelve*, by James D. Nogalski. *CBQ* 58 (1996) 130–31.

Petterson, Anthony R. *Behold Your King: The Hope for the House of David in the Book of Zechariah*. LBHOTS 513. London: T. & T. Clark, 2009.

———. "Exile and Re-Exile in the Twelve." In *Theodicy and Hope in the Book of the Twelve*, edited by George Athas et al., 40–65. LHBOTS 705. London: Bloomsbury T. & T. Clark, 2021.

———. "The Shape of the Davidic Hope across the Book of the Twelve." *JSOT* 35 (2010) 225–46.

Porter, Stanley E. *Sacred Tradition in the New Testament: Tracing Old Testament Themes in the Gospels and Epistles*. Grand Rapids: Baker, 2016.

Portnoy, Stephen L., and David L. Petersen. "Biblical Texts and Statistical Analysis: Zechariah and Beyond." *JBL* 103 (1984) 11–21.

Radday, Yehuda T., and Dieter Wickmann. "The Unity of Zechariah Examined in the Light of Statistical Linguistics." *ZAW* 87 (1975) 30–55.

Redditt, Paul L. "Editorial/Redaction Criticism." In *Dictionary of the Old Testament Prophets*, edited by Mark J. Boda and J. Gordon McConville, 171–78. Downers Grove, IL: IVP Academic, 2012.

Bibliography

———. "The Formation of the Book of the Twelve: A Review of Research." In *Thematic Threads in the Book of the Twelve*, edited by Paul L. Redditt and Aaron Schart, eds., 1–26. BZAW 325. Berlin: de Gruyter, 2003.

———. "The King in Haggai–Zechariah 1–8 and the Book of the Twelve." In *Tradition in Transition: Haggai and Zechariah 1–8 in the Trajectory of Hebrew Theology*, edited by Mark J. Boda and Michael H. Floyd, 56–82. LHBOTS 475. London: T. & T. Clark, 2008.

———. Review of *Literary Precursors to the Book of the Twelve*, by James D. Nogalski and *Redactional Processes in the Book of the Twelve*, by James D. Nogalski. *RevExp* 92 (1995) 105–6.

Redditt, Paul L., and Aaron Schart, eds. *Thematic Threads in the Book of the Twelve*. BZAW 325. Berlin: de Gruyter, 2003.

Rogers, Jeffrey S. Review of *Literary Precursors to the Book of the Twelve*, by James D. Nogalski and *Redactional Processes in the Book of the Twelve*, by James D. Nogalski. *JBL* 114 (1995) 720–22.

Rudman, Dominic. "Zechariah and the Satan Tradition in the Hebrew Bible." In *Tradition in Transition: Haggai and Zechariah 1–8 in the Trajectory of Hebrew Theology*, edited by Mark J. Boda and Michael H. Floyd, 191–209. LHBOTS 475. London: T. & T. Clark, 2008.

Saracco, Norberto. "I Will Pour out My Spirit on All People: A Pastoral Reading of Joel 2:28–30 from Latin America." *CTJ* 46 (2011) 268–77.

Schart, Aaron. *Die Entstehung des Zwölfprophetenbuchs: Neubearbeitungen von Amos im Rahmen schriftenübergreifender Redaktionsprozesse*. BZAW 260. Berlin: de Gruyter, 1998.

———. "The First Section of the Book of the Twelve Prophets: Hosea–Joel–Amos." *Int* 61 (2007) 138–52.

———. "Twelve, Book of the: History of Interpretation." In *Dictionary of the Old Testament Prophets*, edited by Mark J. Boda and J. Gordon McConville, 806–17. Downers Grove, IL: IVP Academic, 2012.

Schneider, D. A. "The Unity of the Book of the Twelve." PhD diss., Yale University, 1979.

Shepherd, Michael B. "Compositional Analysis of the Twelve." *ZAW* 120 (2008) 184–93.

Simkins, Ronald A. "God, History, and the Natural World in the Book of Joel." *CBQ* 55 (1993) 435–52.

Spronk, Klaas. "The Avenging God of Nahum as Comforter of the Traumatized." *AcT* 38 Suppl. 26 (2018) 237–50.

Stovell, Beth M. "Conceptual Metaphor." In *Encyclopedia of Biblical Greek Language and Linguistics*, edited by Stanley E. Porter and Dana Harris. Leiden: Brill (forthcoming).

———. "Ezekiel 34:16: God Feeds His Sheep with Justice." In *Devotions on the Hebrew Bible: 54 Reflections to Inspire and Instruct*, edited by Milton Eng and Lee M. Fields, 79–81. Grand Rapids: Zondervan, 2019.

———. "'I Will Make Her Like a Desert': Intertextual Allusion and Feminine and Agricultural Metaphors in the Book of the Twelve." In *The New Form Criticism and the Book of the Twelve*, edited by Mark J. Boda et al., 37–61. ANEM 10. Atlanta: Society of Biblical Literature Press, 2015.

Stovell, Beth M., and Daniel Timmer. "Introduction." In *Theodicy and Hope in the Book of the Twelve*, edited by George Athas et al., 1–21. LHBOTS 705. London: Bloomsbury T. & T. Clark, 2021.

Strawn, Brent A. *What Is Stronger Than a Lion? Leonine Image and Metaphor in the Hebrew Bible and the Ancient Near East*. OBO 212. Göttingen: Vandenhoeck & Ruprecht, 2005.

Sweeney, Marvin A. "Form and Eschatology in the Book of the Twelve Prophets." In *The New Form Criticism and the Book of the Twelve*, edited by Mark J. Boda et al., 137–61. ANEM 10. Atlanta: Society of Biblical Literature Press, 2015.

———. *Form and Intertextuality in Prophetic and Apocalyptic Literature*. FAT 45. Tübingen: Mohr Siebeck, 2005.

———. "The Place and Function of Joel in the Book of the Twelve." In *Thematic Threads in the Book of the Twelve*, edited by Paul L. Redditt and Aaron Schart, 133–54. BZAW 325. Berlin: de Gruyter, 2003.

———. Review of *Die Entstehung des Zwölfprophetenbuchs: Neubearbeitungen von Amos im Rahmen schriftenübergreifender Redaktionsprozesse*, by Aaron Schart. *Bib* 80 (1999) 279–83.

———. "Swords into Plowshares or Plowshares into Swords? Isaiah and the Twelve in Intertextual Perspective on Zion." *TJT* 34 (2018) 97–110.

———. "Twelve, Book of the." In *Dictionary of the Old Testament Prophets*, edited by Mark J. Boda and J. Gordon McConville, 788–806. Downers Grove, IL: IVP Academic, 2012.

Tanner, Cullen. "Climbing the Lampstand-Witness-Trees: Revelation's Use of Zechariah 4 in Light of Speech Act Theory." *Journal of Pentecostal Theology* 20 (2011) 81–92.

Theocharous, Myrto. *Lexical Dependence and Intertextual Allusion in the Septuagint of the Twelve Prophets: Studies in Hosea, Amos and Micah*. LHBOTS 570. London: Bloomsbury T. & T. Clark, 2012.

Thomas, Heath A. "Hearing the Minor Prophets: The Book of the Twelve and God's Address." In *Hearing the Old Testament: Listening for God's Address*, edited by Craig G. Bartholomew and David J. H. Beldman, 356–79. Grand Rapids: Eerdmans, 2012.

———. "Hope through Human Trafficking? Theodicy in Joel 4:4–8." In *Theodicy and Hope in the Book of the Twelve*, edited by George Athas et al., 88–110. LHBOTS 705. London: Bloomsbury T. & T. Clark, 2021.

Tiemeyer, Lena-Sofia. Review of *Die frühen Sammlungen des Zwölfprophetenbuches: Entstehung und Komposition*, by Jakob Wöhrle and *Der Abschluss des Zwölfprophetenbuches: Buchübergreifende Redaktionsprozesse in den späten Sammlungen*, by Jakob Wöhrle. SEÅ 77 (2012) 373–78.

———. "Zechariah's Spies and Ezekiel's Cherubim." In *Tradition in Transition: Haggai and Zechariah 1–8 in the Trajectory of Hebrew Theology*, edited by Mark J. Boda and Michael H. Floyd, 104–27. LHBOTS 475. London: T. & T. Clark, 2008.

Tiemeyer, Lena-Sofia, and Jakob Wöhrle, eds. *The Book of the Twelve: Composition, Reception, and Interpretation*. VTSup 184. Leiden: Brill, 2020.

Timmer, Daniel C. "'Ah, Assyria Is No More!' Retribution, Theodicy, and Hope in Nahum." In *Theodicy and Hope in the Book of the Twelve*, edited by George Athas et al., 157–72. LHBOTS 705. London: Bloomsbury T. & T. Clark, 2021.

———. *The Non-Israelite Nations in the Book of the Twelve: Thematic Coherence and the Diachronic-Synchronic Relationship in the Minor Prophets*. BibInt 135. Brill: Leiden, 2015.

———. "Where Shall Wisdom Be Found (in the Book of the Twelve)?" In *Riddles and Revelations: Explorations into the Relationship between Wisdom and Prophecy in the Hebrew Bible*, edited by Mark J. Boda et al., 147–63. LHBOTS 634. London: Bloomsbury T. & T. Clark, 2018.

Toffelmire, Colin M. *A Discourse and Register Analysis of the Prophetic Book of Joel*. SSN 66. Leiden: Brill, 2016.

Tuell, Stephen S. "Haggai–Zechariah: Prophecy after the Manner of Ezekiel." In *Thematic Threads in the Book of the Twelve*, edited by Paul L. Redditt and Aaron Schart, 273–91. BZAW 325. Berlin: de Gruyter, 2003.

Van Leeuwen, Raymond. "Cosmos, Temple, House: Building and Wisdom in Ancient Mesopotamia and Israel." In *From the Foundations to the Crenellations: Essays on Temple Building in the Ancient Near East and Hebrew Bible*, edited by Mark J. Boda and Jamie R. Novotny, 399–422. AOAT 366. Münster: Ugarit-Verlag, 2010.

———. "Scribal Wisdom and Theodicy in the Book of the Twelve." In *In Search of Wisdom*, edited by Leo G. Perdue, 31–49. Louisville, KY: Westminster John Knox, 1993.

Watts, John D. W. "A Frame for the Book of the Twelve: Hosea 1–3 and Malachi." In *Reading and Hearing the Book of the Twelve*, edited by James D. Nogalski and Marvin A. Sweeney, 209–17. SymS 15. Atlanta: Society of Biblical Literature Press, 2000.

Werse, Nicholas R. "Joel, Catchwords, and Its Place in the Book of the Twelve." *ZAW* 131 (2019) 549–62.

———. "Obadiah's 'Day of the Lord': A Semiotic Reading." *JSOT* 38 (2013) 109–24.

Weyde, Karl William. Review of *Der Abschluss des Zwölfprophetenbuches: Buchübergreifende Redaktionsprozesse in den späten Sammlungen*, by Jakob Wöhrle. *CBQ* 72 (2010) 363–65.

Wöhrle, Jakob. *Der Abschluss des Zwölfprophetenbuches: Buchübergreifende Redaktionsprozesse in den späten Sammlungen*. BZAW 389. Berlin: de Gruyter, 2008.

———. *Die frühen Sammlungen des Zwölfprophetenbuches: Entstehung und Komposition*. BZAW 360. Berlin: de Gruyter, 2006.

Wright, N. T. *The Day the Revolution Began: Reconsidering the Meaning of Jesus's Crucifixion*. New York: HarperCollins, 2018.

Yates, Gary E. "The Problem of Repentance and Return as a Unifying Theme in the Book of the Twelve." *Them* 41.2 (2016) 248–62.

Young, Ian, Robert Rezetko, and Martin Ehrensvard. *Linguistic Dating of Biblical Texts: An Introduction to Approaches and Problems*. 2 vols. London: Equinox, 2015.

Zapff, Burkhard M. "The Perspective on the Nations in the Book of Micah as a 'Systematization' of the Nations' Role in Joel, Jonah, and Nahum? Reflections on a Context-Oriented Exegesis." In *Thematic Threads in the Book of the Twelve*, edited by Paul L. Redditt and Aaron Schart, 292–312. BZAW 325. Berlin: de Gruyter, 2003.

AUTHOR INDEX

Abernethy, A. T., 32n7-8, 33n9-12
Albertz, R., 22, 23, 26
Allen, L. C., 119n19
Andiñach, P. R., 75n12, 76n15, 76n18
Athas, G., 44n54-55, 47n64, 48n70, 110n1, 115n13, 116n15, 126n35-37

Bakon, S., 75n9, 76n14
Barker, J. D., 73n6, 74n7, 88n58
Bartholomew, C., 138n18
Beker, J. C., 111
Belibtreu, E., 121n23
Ben Zvi, E., 160-63
Bergmann, C. D., 119n21, 120n22
Bergmann, N. W., 105n37, 106n38-40
Biddle, M. E., 26
Boadt, L., 31n2, 31n4

Boda, M. J., 20, 21, 22n47-50, 24, 47n65, 47n67, 55n8, 55n10, 56n13-14, 61n26, 62n31, 64n36, 65n37, 68n45, 83n44, 84n45-47, 84n49, 85n50-51, 94n6, 101n25, 124, 125
Boloje, B. O., 85n53, 86n54-55
Bowman, C., 53n3, 54n6, 55n7
Braaten, L. J., 93n2, 94n5, 95n8-9, 106n41-42, 107n43
Bulkeley, T., 78n27-28

Clark, D. A. R., 96n11, 97n12-14
Clendenen, E. R., 137
Creach, J. F. D., 84n48
Crenshaw, J. L., 23
Cruz, J., 134n10

De Moor, J. C., 111n2

Author Index

De Roche, M., 96n10
De Vries, S. J., 22, 23
Delkurt, H., 26
Dines, J., 133
Dodd, C. H., 89n60

Ehrensvard, M., 137n13
Erickson, M. J., 72n4, 89–90n60
Evans, C. A., 27

Floyd, M. H., 24, 122n28, 123n30
Flynn, S. W., 31n6
Fox, N. S., 30n1, 31n5
Fuller, D. J., 123n29, 137

Gärtner, J., 26
Goswell, G., 32n7–8, 33n9–12, 34n13, 35n19–20, 36n22–25, 37n26, 37n28–29, 38n30–32, 39n33–36, 40n37, 41n41–45, 42n46, 43n48–49, 45n56, 45n59–60, 46n61–63, 120n22
Green, M., 138n16
Grenz, S. J., 72n4, 73n4
Groenewald, A., 85n53, 86n54–55

Habel, N. C., 104n33
Hays, R. B., 89n59
Hecke, P. van, 4n6, 48n71
Hoffman, Y., 71n3, 82n38
House, P. R., 15, 16, 24, 53n1, 55n11, 58n19, 60n22, 60n24, 61n27, 61n30, 63n34, 64n35, 65n38, 66n40, 68n47, 75n10–11, 75n13, 76n20, 78n29, 79n30, 82n39–41, 83n42, 85n52, 87n56, 132

Ishai-Rosenboim, D., 71n1–2

Jeremias, J., 75n8, 76n21, 77n22
Jerome, 4
Johnson, M., 133, 134n6
Jones, P., 31n3

Kelle, B. E., 54n4, 134n8–9
Kessler, R., 118n18
Kim, B., 93, 112n5, 113, 114n9–10
King, A. M., 104n32
Ko, G., 114n11, 119n19, 122n27
Krispenz, J., 140

Laato, A., 111n2
Lakoff, G., 133, 134
Lancaster, M. D., 134n7, 141
Larkin, K. J. A., 141
LeCureux, J. T., 15, 16n11–13, 55n9, 56n12, 57n15, 67n42–43, 68n46, 147n9, 147n11–12
Lessing, R. R., 99n18–19, 100n20–22, 101n23–24
Loya, M. T., 105n34–36
Lust, J., 152n25, 153n27–28, 154n31, 154n33–34, 154n36

Macintosh, A. A., 140n24
Mak, C. D., 117n17
Mayhue, R., 73n5, 77n24, 83n43
Meyers, C. L., 45n57, 48n72, 49n76, 50n77–78

Author Index

Meyers, E. M., 45n57, 48n72, 49n76, 50n77–78
Mitchell, C., 97n15, 98n16
Muller-Lopez, K., 134n11

Nogalski, J. D., 3n2, 3–4n3, 4n5, 14–20, 23, 51n80, 76n17, 77n23, 78n25–26, 79n31–32, 80n33–35, 93n4, 95n7, 102n26–27, 103n28, 111n4, 145, 146, 148–53, 155–56, 159–62, 164

O'Brien, J. M., 134n9, 149n15, 149n17, 150n19, 151n21
O'Dowd, R., 138n18

Petersen, D. L., 136n12
Petterson, A. R., 34n15–16, 35n17–18, 36n21, 37n27, 40n38, 42n47, 43n50, 47n66–67, 48n68–69, 48n72, 49n73–75, 50n79, 113n7, 114n12, 119, 120n22, 122n26
Porter, S. E., 133n3
Portnoy, S. L., 136n12

Radday, Y. T., 136n12
Redditt, P. L., 22, 24–26, 43n53, 144n1–3, 145n4, 146n6–7, 148n13, 149n16, 153n30
Rendtorff, R., 16
Rezetko, R., 137n13
Rogers, J. S., 150n18, 151n20
Rudman, D., 25

Saracco, N., 117n16
Schart, A., 22, 57n16, 59n21, 146, 152–56, 159, 160, 162, 164
Schneider, D. A., 146–48, 162, 164
Shepherd, M. B., 145n5
Simkins, R. A., 99n17
Spronk, K., 121n24
Stovell, B. M., 20, 48n71, 92n1, 110n1, 111n2, 134n6
Strawn, B. A., 103n29–31, 104n32
Sweeney, M. A., 16, 20, 21, 23, 34n14, 87n57, 130, 131n1, 133, 147n8, 147n10, 152n24, 152n26, 153n29, 154n32, 154n35, 154n37–39

Tanner, C., 138
Theocharous, M., 133
Thomas, H. A., 18, 19, 21, 23, 115n14
Tiemeyer, L., 25, 26, 156n41–43, 157n45–47, 157n50–51, 158n53–55
Timmer, D. C., 40n39–40, 43n51–52, 110n1, 111n2, 121n25, 139
Toffelmire, C. M., 110n1, 137
Trudinger, P., 104n33
Tuell, S. S., 23, 24n60

Van Leeuwen, R., 139n19, 141

Watts, J. D. W., 16, 17n17–19
Werse, N. R., 76n16, 76n19, 81n37

Weyde, K. W., 157n44, 157n46, 157n48–49, 158n52
Wickmann, D., 136n12
Wöhrle, J., 26, 146, 152, 155–60, 162, 164
Wright, N. T., 89n60

Yates, G. E., 54n5, 58n17–18, 59n20, 60n23, 61n25, 61n28–29, 62n32, 63n33, 66n39, 67n41
Young, I., 137n13

Zapff, B. M., 24

SCRIPTURE INDEX

OLD TESTAMENT

Genesis

	96, 133
1	96
1:20a	96
1:20b	96
1:24	96
1:26	96, 97
3:9	52
9:11	96
9:15	96
9:17	105
49:8–12	4

Exodus

	58
21:24–25	80n36
28:36–38	85
32–34	57
32:11–14	58
32:12	58, 61
32:14	58
34:1–4	57
34:5–7	57
34:6–7	18, 61, 62, 120, 145
34:6	58, 116, 158
40:38	39

Leviticus

11:1–8	101
24:20	80n36

Numbers

23:21–24	4

Scripture Index

Deuteronomy

	105, 113
6:4	84
17:14–20	31
19:21	80n36
20:16–18	84n48
28:15–68	93
28:38–40	105
28:49–51	105

Judges

5:4–5	98, 99
10:4	46
12:14	46

1 Samuel

	33
8:4–8	31
13:14	31

2 Samuel

	33
6	39
6:1–15	31
7:5–7	32
7:9	32
7:10–11	32
7:11	32
7:12	40
7:13	32
7:14	32
7:15	32
7:16	32
8:15	32

1 Kings

	33
1:13	46
1:38	46
1:44	46

1 Chronicles

	33
21	25

Job

	131, 139
1–2	25

Psalms

	31, 33
1	138
2	33
18:35	46
29:10	31
41	33
45:4	46
72	33
89–90	33
89:49	33
90:1–2	33
96:10	31
104:2	97

Proverbs

	131, 138, 140
1	138

Scripture Index

Ecclesiastes

	131, 138

Isaiah

	2, 133, 161
2:12–22	82
4:4–6	39
4:6	39
9:6	41
11:1	41
26:11	42
34:8	74
42:5	97
60:19	84

Jeremiah

	2, 161
22:24–30	43, 44
22:24–25	43
23:5–6	47
33:15–16	47

Ezekiel

	2, 24, 25, 161
3	122
7:19	74
33	122
34	48n71

Hosea

	1–3, 5, 10, 14, 15, 20–25, 30, 34–37, 53–56, 59, 62, 64–68, 92, 93, 103, 104, 112–14, 116, 119, 120, 124–28, 134, 141, 147, 148, 151–53, 155–56, 158, 159
1–3	16, 54
1:1	143, 148
1:2	54
1:2b	95
1:5	22
1:7	24
1:9	36
1:10—2:1	114
1:10–11	35, 36, 50
1:10	35
1:11	24, 36
2–3	113
2	54n4, 92
2:2	54
2:4–5	113
2:5	112
2:6	54
2:7	54
2:7a	54
2:7b	93
2:8–9	92
2:9	54
2:14–15	114
2:22–23	114
2:23	21, 36
3:1–5	23
3:1–3	36
3:1	16, 113
3:4–5	17, 21, 54
3:4	36
3:5	16, 24, 36, 37, 50, 55, 60
4:1	153
4:1b–2	104

Scripture Index

Hosea (continued)

4:3	104, 105, 112
4:12–14	113
5:1	35
5:4	16, 55
5:7b	22
5:14–15	4
5:14	103
5:15	37
5:16	37
6:1	55
6:3–11	55
6:3a	55
6:7	113
7:9	112
7:10	37
8:1	113
8:2	21
8:4	35
8:7	112
8:12	113
8:13	15
9:7	35
9:11–14	20
9:11	20
9:13	20
9:14	20
10	113
10:13	113
11	55
11:5b	55
11:7a	55
11:8–9	56, 103
11:8	55
11:9a	55
11:10	4, 103
11:11	103
12	56
12:1–5	56
12:6	56
13	56
13:7–8	4, 103
14	114
14:1–2	67
14:1–2a	56, 57
14:2–4	23
14:3	21, 56
14:4–7	56
14:4	56
14:5–8	114
14:6–7	93
14:9	19

Joel

	1, 14, 34, 38, 57–62, 64–67, 69, 73, 75–78, 80, 87, 88, 94, 100–102, 104–6, 112, 115–20, 126–28, 133, 137, 145–51, 154–60
1–3	115
1–2	76, 102
1	59, 75, 76, 106
1:2—2:17	94, 146
1:2—2:11	57
1:2–12	75
1:2–5	116
1:2	106
1:4	115
1:5	106
1:6a	105
1:8	106
1:10	106
1:10a	105
1:11	106
1:13–14	75
1:13	106, 115

Scripture Index

Reference	Pages
1:15	75, 80
1:19–20	75
1:19	107
2	61, 98
2:1–11	75
2:1	80
2:2	78, 149, 150
2:10–11	76
2:10	98, 99
2:11b	75
2:12–17	75
2:12–14	57, 60, 115
2:12–13	67
2:12	60, 116
2:13	58, 60, 116, 145, 158
2:13b	57
2:14	58, 61
2:14a	60
2:15–17	57, 58
2:15–16	58
2:17	62, 115
2:17b	58
2:18—3:21	57
2:18–27	75
2:18	94
2:19–26	58
2:21a	94
2:22	94
2:24	116
2:25	115, 116
2:27	58
2:28–32	73, 117
2:28–29	65, 76, 117
2:28	65, 75, 76
2:31	75
2:32	75
3	38
3:4–8	115n14
3:10	150
3:12	76
3:14	80
3:15–16a	76, 98
3:16	4, 38, 99, 145
3:17–18	76
3:17	76
3:18	38
3:18a	78
3:20	76

Amos

Reference	Pages
	1–5, 10, 14, 23–25, 30, 34, 37–40, 59–60, 62, 66–68, 77–79, 87–88, 99–101, 112, 117–18, 120, 126–28, 145, 147–59
1–2	45n58, 153
1:1	37, 99, 149, 152
1:2	4, 37, 38, 145, 153
2	118
2:4–5	153
2:6	118
2:10–12	153
3–6	152
3:1	153
3:1b	153
3:7	153
3:15	99
4	59
4:6–11	37, 153
4:6	59
4:8	59
4:9	59, 154
4:10	59
4:11	59

Amos (continued)

Reference	Page
4:12b	59
4:13	154
5	59, 118
5:2	40
5:4–14	38
5:4	59
5:5	60
5:6	59
5:7	60
5:8	154
5:12	77
5:14	60, 77
5:15	60
5:15b	60
5:18–20	60, 77, 78
5:18	77, 78
5:20	77, 78
6:4–7	38
6:5	37, 38
6:11	99
7–9	153
7:9	39
7:13	39
8	78, 118
8:4–7	153
8:4–6	78
8:8	99
8:9–13	78
8:9	78, 99
8:10	78
8:11–12	78
8:13–14	78
8:14	40
9	118
9:1	39, 99
9:5	99
9:6	154
9:7–10	23, 153
9:8–10	78
9:11–15	24, 78
9:11	37–40, 50, 78, 154, 157
9:12	38–40, 154
9:12b	154, 157
9:13	38
9:13a	154
9:13b	78, 154
9:14–15	154
9:14	38
9:15	39

Obadiah

Reference	Page
	1, 2n1, 14, 21, 34, 39, 40, 79–81, 87, 88, 147–49, 151, 154, 155, 157, 159, 161
1:1–9	79
1:8–9	80
1:10–14	79, 80
1:11–14	79
1:11	79
1:12–14	79, 80
1:14a	79
1:15–21	161
1:15–18	80
1:15–16	79
1:15	79
1:17–21	80
1:17	39
1:17a	157
1:18	80
1:19	40
1:20	40

Scripture Index

Jonah

	1, 14, 34, 60–62, 67, 135, 145, 147–51, 154–55, 158–61
2	151
2:4	151
2:7	151
3:4	60
3:7	60
3:8b	60
3:9	60, 61
3:10	61
4	151
4:2	61, 145, 158
4:11	61

Micah

	1, 3, 5, 10, 14–16, 20–26, 30, 34, 40–42, 62, 63, 66, 67, 112, 118–20, 126–28, 133, 134, 147–61
1	119, 151
1:1–7	161
1:1	149
1:2—2:11	119
1:8	119
1:15–16	119
2:12–13	24, 119
2:12	41
2:13	41
3:1	153
3:12	21
4–5	24, 26
4	38
4:1–4	157
4:2b	38
4:3	150
4:6	41
4:7	41
4:8	42, 157
4:9–10	20, 24, 41
4:9	119
4:10	41, 119
4:11–13	41
4:13	41
5:1–4	40, 50, 157
5:2	21, 41, 42
5:3	119
5:4	41
5:5	41
5:6	21
5:7–9	41
5:7	41
5:9–13	23
5:9	42
5:10–14	119
5:15	119
6:6–8	62
6:6b–7	62
6:6	62
6:7	62
6:8	62
7:9	62
7:10	62
7:18–20	158
7:18–19	120
7:18–19a	62
7:18	145

Nahum

	1, 14, 15, 21, 34, 60–63, 67, 100, 112, 120–22, 127, 128, 135, 139, 143, 146–51, 154–56, 159, 160
1	121, 146, 154
1:1	143
1:2–3	120, 145, 158
1:5	100
2	121
2:2	121
3	102
3:1–3	121
3:15a	102
3:15b	102
3:17a	102

Habakkuk

	1, 14, 15, 21, 22, 34, 63, 67, 112, 119, 122–25, 128, 137, 139, 146, 147, 149, 151, 154, 155, 157, 159, 160
1–2	122, 123, 144
1:2	122
1:3	122
1:4	122
1:9b	102
2	122, 123
2:1	122
2:20	22, 125
3	123, 144, 146, 154
3:1	143
3:6	123
3:13	34
3:17–18	123
3:19	123, 129

Zephaniah

	1, 5, 10, 14, 15, 22–26, 34, 62–63, 66–67, 81–82, 87–88, 96–97, 124–25, 147–51, 153, 155, 156, 159
1–2	97
1	97
1:1	149
1:2	81
1:2–3	96
1:3	96
1:3b	96
1:4–6	23, 81
1:7	22, 81
1:9	81
1:14	81
1:15	81, 149, 150
1:17a	125
1:18	81
2	97
2:1–3	82
2:1	82
2:2	82
2:3	63, 82
2:4–15	82
2:14	96
3	26, 97
3:1–7	82

Scripture Index

3:8	82
3:9–13	82
3:11–13	23
3:14–20	24, 82
3:14	125
3:15	34
3:16	82

Haggai

	1, 5, 14, 15, 24, 30, 34, 42–47, 63–64, 67, 100, 124, 125, 144, 147–49, 151, 154–56, 159
1:1	144
1:2–11	63
1:6	94, 146
1:10–11	94, 146
1:12	63
1:13	63
1:14	63
1:15—2:1	144
2	100
2:6–9	43
2:6–7	100
2:7–9	63
2:7	43
2:10	144
2:20–23	25, 42, 43, 51
2:20	144
2:21	100
2:22–23	43
2:22	43, 100
2:23	42, 43, 100

Zechariah

	2, 2n1, 5, 24, 30, 34, 44–51, 64–68, 83–88, 94, 97, 101, 112, 124–28, 133, 134, 138, 141, 144, 147–51, 154–57, 159
1–8	14, 24, 144, 147–49, 151
1–6	25, 26
1:1	144
1:3	64, 65, 67
1:4–6a	64
1:6b	64
1:7	144
1:16a	64
2	125
2:10	45, 125
2:11–12	157
2:13	22, 125
2:15	83
3	25, 47, 48
3:6–8	126
3:8	25, 47
3:9	50
3:10	25, 83
4	46
4:1–7	46
4:6–10a	25
4:6	126
4:8–10	46
4:11–13	46
4:14	46
6:11	47
6:12–13	47
6:12	25
7	64

Zechariah (continued)

7:1	144
8	151
8:3	45
8:9–12	94
8:12	94
8:16–17	64
8:18–23	64
8:23	83
9–14	25, 124, 141, 147–51
9	45, 125
9:1–10	24
9:1–7	45
9:4	45
9:7	45
9:8	45, 46
9:9–10	44–48, 50
9:9	44–46, 48, 49, 51, 125
9:10	157
9:13	150
9:16	83
10–11	49
10:3–4	48
10:4	51
11	49
12–13	66
12	97
12:1	97
12:3	83, 97
12:4	83
12:6	83, 97
12:7–9	49
12:7	49
12:8	49, 83
12:9	83
12:10–14	51
12:10	49, 50, 65
12:11–14	65
12:11	83
12:12	49
13:1	65, 83
13:2–6	65
13:2	83
13:4	83
13:7–8	49
13:9	49
14	45, 83, 151
14:1–2	83
14:1	83
14:3–5	84
14:5	101
14:7	84
14:8	84
14:9	84
14:10	84
14:11	84
14:12–15	84
14:13a	84
14:14	84
14:16–19	84
14:20–21	101
14:20	84, 101
14:21b	85

Malachi

	1, 2, 5, 14–18, 21, 35, 65
1	151
1:2	16
1:6	126
1:9	158
1:11–12	126
3:1–5	86
3:1–3	127
3:1	35, 85
3:2	85
3:3–4	21, 85
3:4	127

3:5	16, 85
3:6	17
3:7	65, 68
3:8–15	66
3:8–10	95
3:11	95, 102
3:16	66
3:17	86
3:18	17
4:1	66
4:1a	86
4:2	86
4:3	86
4:4–6	158, 159
4:4	66
4:5–6	21
4:5	66, 86
4:6	66, 86
4:6b	95

NEW TESTAMENT

Matthew

2:6	40
21:5	44

Mark

11:15	85

John

12:15	44

Acts

2	89
2:14–24	73

Romans

2:5	73
2:16	73

1 Corinthians

1:8	73
5:5	73

2 Corinthians

1:14	73

Philippians

1:6	73

1 Thessalonians

5:2–3	73

2 Thessalonians

2:2–3	73

2 Timothy

4:8	73

2 Peter

2:9	73
3:10	73

Revelation

	138
6:12–14	101
18:4	52

RABBINIC SOURCES

b. B. Bat.

13b–15a	3n3

www.ingramcontent.com/pod-product-compliance
Lightning Source LLC
Chambersburg PA
CBHW031427150426
43191CB00006B/436